ESSENTIAL
AUSTIN-HEALEY
100 & 3000

ESSENTIAL
AUSTIN-HEALEY
100 & 3000

THE CARS AND THEIR STORY
1953-67

MIKE LAWRENCE

BAY VIEW
BOOKS

Published 1994 by Bay View Books Ltd
The Red House, 25-26 Bridgeland Street,
Bideford, Devon EX39 2PZ

© Copyright 1994 by Bay View Books Ltd
Edited by Mark Hughes
Designed by Peter Laws
Computer make-up by Chris Fayers

ISBN 1 870979 49 4
Printed in Hong Kong

CONTENTS

BIRTH OF THE 100

Donald Mitchell Healey was born in Perranporth, Cornwall in 1898, the son of a prosperous builder who was also a pioneer motorist. He was apprenticed to the aircraft maker, Sopwith, which was based at the Brooklands circuit, so he was exposed to motor racing at a young age. Healey was 16 when World War I broke out and, when he was old enough, he enlisted as a pilot in the Royal Flying Corps. He later regretted the decision because the £200 his father had paid for his apprenticeship included flying lessons, and he later said that had he completed his time with Sopwith there would have been Healey aircraft rather than Healey cars.

After crashing a 'plane, he was invalided out of the RFC and returned to his native Cornwall, where he opened a garage and for a time made wireless sets. By the time he was in his early 20s, Healey had demonstrated skill in motor sport, courage, engineering prowess and talent as an entrepreneur with an eye on the next opportunity. He was not unaware of his abilities and could sometimes be a blunt, forthright man.

In the 1920s Healey began to compete in hill climbs and trials, and in 1928 he won the first RAC Rally. Encouraged by this, he drove a Triumph in the 1929 Monte Carlo Rally, which was then the toughest rally in the world. He failed to qualify as a finisher, but the following year he was seventh overall and first Brit home. He won in 1931, and in later events he took a second, a third and a class win. He also won Alpine Cups in three successive Alpine Rallies to become the most successful British rally driver of the 1930s. It is no coincidence that Healey's cars were to gain their greatest successes in rallying and what was, for a long time, its close relative on the track: classic long-distance sports car racing.

Healey's sporting successes, allied with his engineering skills and personality, opened doors for him. In 1930 he joined Invicta, where he helped design the superb 4½-litre S-type low-chassis model. Then he had a spell at Riley before moving to Triumph in 1933. Before long he was Triumph's Technical Director and responsible for a new range of engines, including a double overhead camshaft straight-eight which owed more than a little to Alfa Romeo. Healey left for a short period with Lucas before returning to Triumph in 1937 as a member of the board.

Triumphs built under Healey's direction were generally well received. Rather like Jaguars, they offered a lot of style and performance for the money, but tooling costs for new models ate into the profits and in 1939 the company went into receivership. Healey tried to buy Triumph, but it went to Thomas Ward, an engineering group. He stayed on for a time as General Manager before moving to Humber to work on armoured cars.

While at Humber, Healey met two men who shared his ideas for a new range of sporting cars to be built after the war: Achille 'Sammy' Sampietro, who had worked for Alfa Romeo and Maserati, and Ben Bowden, who had been a stylist with Farina (the original company of which Pininfarina is an off-shoot). During the war, they conceived a design which they tried to sell to Triumph. When Triumph finally decided against it, Healey went into production on his own account using tuned 2½-litre Riley engines.

The Donald Healey Motor Company (DHM) was established on £20,000 invested by Donald and his father, and the first car was completed in 1945 in a corner of a factory which made concrete mixers. The following year the company went into production in Warwick making handsome roadsters, sports cars and saloons. Each had a rigid box-section chassis weighing only 160lb, front suspension by trailing arms, and an aerodynamically-efficient body. For the first products from a small company, the cars were remarkable. The Elliot saloon of 1948, for example, was officially timed

The very first Healey, built at Warwick in 1946, was a Westland Roadster. Its proud creators were (from left) Achille 'Sammy' Sampietro, Donald Healey and Ben Bowden.

Healey's early products were remarkable. Officially timed at 110.8mph, the Elliot saloon of 1948 was then the fastest four-seat production car in the world.

The Silverstone was a sports two-seater designed for road and track. Although outclassed by lighter and more powerful rivals, this Healey model was a popular choice for club racers. This is A.J.A. Stokes approaching Copse Corner at, appropriately, Silverstone circuit.

at 110.8mph, which made it the fastest four-seat production car in the world. Donald Healey, co-driving with his son Geoffrey, was ninth in the 1948 Mille Miglia with a Healey Roadster, while a Healey saloon took two class wins in the same race. The following year Geoffrey, co-driving with Tommy Wisdom, entered the Mille Miglia again and brought a Westland Roadster home tenth, winning its class.

A sports two-seater, the Silverstone, enjoyed success as a dual-purpose road and competition car, although it was on the heavy side at 19cwt and was out-classed in racing by the lighter and more powerful Bristol-engined Frazer Nash Le Mans Replica. The

apex of the Silverstone's competition career was second overall and first in class for Donald Healey/Tommy Wisdom in the 1949 Alpine Rally and a win in the 1950 production car race at Silverstone. Healey Silverstones ran at Le Mans in 1949 and 1950, but they were out-paced by cars with smaller engines. Still, it was with a Healey Silverstone that the great Tony Brooks made a name in British club racing in what was supposed to be his mother's 'shopping car'.

Healey had stolen a march by getting his cars into production so soon after the war, but the Riley engine was a pre-war design and was beginning to show its age. Further, prevailing economic conditions made life difficult for specialist car makers. Purchase tax in Britain was levied at 33% of the basic price, less the dealer's mark-up, but if the basic was over £1000 the tax doubled. Jaguar managed to bring the XK120 to the market at a basic £998, but a Healey Roadster, being hand-built, cost a basic £1500, which meant there was an additional £834 16s 8d to pay in purchase tax. Like most small constructors, Healey

Anglo-American partnership: using Nash running gear and a chassis based on the Healey Silverstone, the Nash-Healey was sold only in North America. This is the early body design, later superseded by a sleeker shape from Pinin Farina.

When Donald Healey schemed his new low-cost 100mph sports car, he discovered an inexpensive source of components, including a 2660cc four-cylinder engine, in the slow-selling Austin A90 Atlantic.

stayed in business because new cars were so scarce that it was a seller's market, but that was to change when the government decided to ease a number of restrictions in 1952.

In 1949 Donald Healey was travelling to America on the the *Queen Elizabeth* when he met George Romney, General Manager of the Nash-Kelvinator Corporation. Nash had prospered during the war when engaged on government work, but was facing the problem of competing with the Detroit Big Three

in peacetime. The two car-makers discussed the problem and the Nash-Healey was born. Healey would supply Nash with chassis based on the Silverstone, with enveloping bodies, while Nash would provide the running gear. The idea was to cash in on the sports car boom which was hitting America, and to have glamorous cars in the showrooms to attract attention and raise Nash's profile.

The Nash-Healey was not a success. Its styling was bland and it could not compete with the Jaguar

XK120 on looks, price or performance. Nash had it restyled by Pinin Farina (it was later that the company became 'Pininfarina'), but even so total production was only 506 and Nash made a loss on every one. With hindsight, Nash should have taken over the design and mass-produced to a price, the formula which Austin was to use with such success. Still, Nash-Healeys prepared and entered by the Donald Healey Motor Company came third in the Le Mans 24 Hours in 1950 and 1952.

Nash-Healeys were sold only in North America, but a similar car was offered in Britain with a 3-litre Alvis engine. It was not a success and the fact that 25 were sold was solely due to there being a seller's market. Although the ambitious project with Nash had been a failure, it had introduced Healey to the North American market and had given him considerable food for thought.

At the end of 1951, Donald and Geoffrey Healey began work on a new low-cost sports car, pitched between the MG TD and Jaguar XK120. It was intended to be the first reasonably priced sports car to offer 100mph performance, and the American market was firmly in mind. Austin agreed to supply running gear from the A90 Atlantic sports saloon/cabriolet and was glad to do so because the Atlantic had not been selling well.

Austin was controlled by Leonard Lord, who had worked for Lord Nuffield (William Morris) until they fell out and Lord left. Pre-war the British car market had been dominated by Austin and the Nuffield Group (Morris, MG, Riley and Wolseley), but in the late 1940s they came under increasing pressure from Ford and Vauxhall, which were American-owned. It became clear that a merger was desirable and it finally happened in November 1951 when Austin and the Nuffield Group combined to form the British Motor Corporation. It was not an easy marriage and for many years, even into the 1970s, there was rivalry between the Austin and Nuffield sides. Lord promoted his Austin side, which retained a separate dealer network, and he encouraged some specialist makers to build an Austin-powered sports car which would rival Nuffield's MG.

This was understood to be an unofficial competition and Jensen responded with a rakish car using 1.2-litre Austin A40 components (Jensen made the bodies for the stodgey Austin A40 'Sports', which looked like a miniature Jensen Interceptor). The other two competitors, Healey and Frazer Nash, chose components from the Austin A90 Atlantic, an ill-conceived car which had been aimed at America and fallen short of the target. A sports car which used Atlantic components made economic sense since the Atlantic would be axed in 1952 and a new car would absorb redundant components. Further, Donald Healey moved in motor industry circles, and knew the Austin/Nuffield merger was in the air before it occurred. When that happened, he expected that there would be rationalisation, that the Riley engine was a strong candidate for axing, and that his supply of engines would soon disappear.

Geoffrey Healey and Barrie Bilbie designed the chassis of the new car, while Gerry Coker, who had joined Healey from Rootes in 1950, did the styling. Sales of perhaps 20 a week were hoped for, although it would take some time to reach this figure since the Donald Healey Motor Company could not make more than five cars a week in 1951. Named the Healey Hundred (it had a top speed of just over 100mph and proved it by making a two-way run at 106.05mph on the Jabbeke-Aeltre *autoroute* in Belgium), it was the sensation of the 1952 London Motor Show and completely over-shadowed Triumph's ungainly prototype which would, with development, become the TR2. It also over-shadowed the modified 'Targa Florio' with A90 running gear shown by Frazer Nash. The Jensen entry in Leonard Lord's unofficial competition did not make the Motor Show because it was missing some components, and it remained a footnote to the history of the British sports car.

Tail fins were in fashion and the Healey Hundred had them during the build process, but Donald disliked them so much that the rear panels were changed while the prototype was being bodied at Tickford. When the prototype was finished, the radiator grille was also not quite right. It was similar to the grille on the production 100, but was not as sharply defined. When the car was put on its little stand at the Motor Show, a day late, Healey ordered that the nose be set against a pillar so it could not be seen clearly. It made no difference and the car drew the crowds, one journalist commenting that it was just as well it was placed against a pillar because the public would otherwise have swamped it. This overwhelmingly favourable reaction clinched the matter for Leonard Lord, who had been kept informed

The prototype Healey Hundred established a family look that was to survive for 15 years. Only details, such as the height of the headlamps, were altered for the production 100.

From the rear, the prototype Hundred is recognised by its distinctive steel disc wheels and the lack of a boot lid badge. Notice that the car, firmly aimed at the American market, is left-hand drive.

11

The prototype in rolling chassis form, photographed just before it left Healey's Warwick works for the body to be fitted by Tickford in Newport Pagnell. Interesting details are the stoutness of the scuttle area, the rear suspension Panhard rod and the twin six-volt batteries.

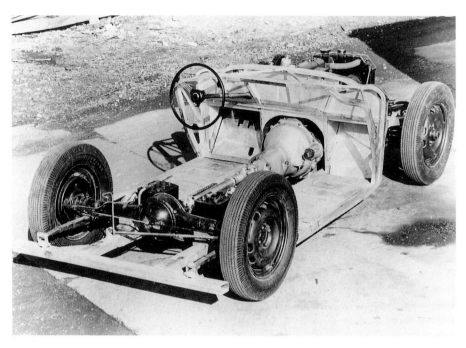

The prototype Hundred's four-cylinder Austin engine of 2660cc, but at this stage the badge and chassis plate just say 'Healey'. The peak at the top of the radiator grille was flattened off for production versions.

received during the Motor Show alone and DHM had never made more than 200 cars in any one year. Lord invited Healey to dinner that night and before the meal was over Austin had bought the rights to the Healey Hundred. The car was re-badged 'Austin-Healey' while it sat on its stand at the Motor Show and the Donald Healey Motor Company was engaged as consultants on a 20-year contract. DHM would develop new designs and special projects such as competition versions of production cars.

There is a story that Healey had priced the car at £850 and that Lord, knowing the economies which could be effected by mass-production, reduced it to £750. In fact, these were targets and no official price was announced until the car entered production.

The prototype next appeared at the Miami World's Fair, where it won the Grand Premier Award, and at the 1953 New York Show it was voted International Show Car of the Year. It created excitement everywhere it appeared.

Meanwhile, Austin hastily prepared the car for production and Lord continued to play the corporate game. The MGA could have entered the market before the Austin-Healey, but MG was forced to soldier on with the TF, a lightly revised TD. It was a case of Lord promoting his baby at the expense of the ex-Nuffield makes, and one effect was that Triumph took sales from MG.

of developments. The story that Lord came across the car at the Motor Show and fell in love at first sight is sheer fantasy.

Healey was deluged with orders and it was clear that he could not meet them: over 3000 orders were

Austin-Healey became an established and successful marque, but it was to be a neglected one. When the last car to bear the name was made, there had not been a completely new design since the Sprite 13 years earlier. The original Healey Hundred had been developed, but it had never been re-designed and nor was there a fresh design to replace it. BMC had an endless list of problems which mainly sprung from bad management, it underwent a series of takeovers and mergers, and it failed to keep pace with new safety and emission laws introduced in the USA. The Big Healey was killed off at the end of 1967 and the new laws were offered as the excuse, but the three examples of the Austin-Healey 4000 made by DHM met American requirements.

For various reasons, dealt with in a later chapter, the Austin-Healey 4000 did not go ahead. The arrangement with the Donald Healey Motor Company was ended prematurely and the last 8443 Austin-Healey Sprites were sold as 'Austins', a name which did not have the same cachet. Production of the Sprite ended in 1971 even though the similar MG Midget continued until 1979.

Donald Healey still wanted to build cars and found a new partner in Jensen, which had built the bodies for the Big Healeys and had spare capacity when that contract ended. Healey developed the Jensen-Healey sports car, but it disappointed: its 16-valve Lotus

The original Healey Hundred on test in Belgium with *Autosport*'s John Bolster. With windscreen folded, Bolster reached 106mph along the Jabbeke autoroute, scene of many speed runs.

engine gave many problems on the early cars, it suffered from scuttle shake, and rust was endemic. In a four-year production life, 1972-76, the total of 10,926 Jensen-Healeys made was way below target. A further 473 Jensen GTs were made in 1975-76, but by that time Healey had severed his links with Jensen and his name did not appear on the car. Jensen went into receivership late in 1975 and eventually closed the following May.

In 1974 the Donald Healey Motor Company was sold to the Hamblin Group (it exists today as a car dealer) while another firm, Healey Automobile Consultants Ltd, remained independent and worked on a number of design projects. There was also Healey Marine, an ill-starred effort to build boats.

Donald Healey died on 15 January 1988 at the age of 89. He left an impressive legacy of automotive design from the Invicta S-type, via the Triumph Dolomite to the car which will be remembered as long as motor cars are remembered, the Big Healey. His son, Geoffrey, outlived him by only six years and died on 29 April 1994.

THE RANGE IN BRIEF

Once the decision to make the Austin-Healey 100 was made, a batch of 20 cars was hand-built by Tickford between October 1952 and February 1953. These had aluminium panels although many contemporary reports wrongly called them 'light alloy' (aluminium is an element, not an alloy). Tickford did not have the capacity to meet the planned output of 150-200 cars a week and the contract for assembling the bodies (many of the panels came from Boulton Paul, better known for aircraft) and chassis (from Thompsons of Wolverhampton) went to Jensen, which was some compensation for having failed to interest Austin in its A40-based sports car. As it happened, 200 cars a week were never made and usually the figure hovered around the 100 mark, plus or minus 20.

Production began at the Austin factory at Longbridge in May 1953. Over the next 14 years,

88.8% of all Big Healeys would go to North America, just 5.9% would be sold on the home market, and the rest would be distributed mainly around the Commonwealth and, later, a few European countries – or so it is thought. In fact, even the most assiduous researchers have not been able to set their findings in stone because the Longbridge records are vague. Only after production moved to the MG plant in Abingdon in 1957 were reliable records kept. Within the Big Healey's production total of 72,027 cars, 234 were supplied in CKD (Completely Knocked Down) kits for assembly by BMC's overseas subsidiaries. This was a device to circumvent import restrictions and, in theory, an Austin agency in some remote outpost could have accepted and assembled a CKD kit.

As sold in 1953, the 100 differed very little from the prototype, the changes amounting to a slightly raised headlight height, a revised grille with a sharper

At speed in an Austin-Healey 100 finished in Old English White. In BN1 form, the 100's three-speed gearbox was augmented by overdrive on the top two ratios.

outline, and a couple of minor mechanical details. Many writers have claimed that this demonstrates that Healey's concept was right from the start, but the rush to put an untried prototype into production in a matter of months meant that the car had serious flaws, such as scuttle shake, a steering column which could kill a driver in a head-on shunt, excessive engine heat permeating into the cockpit, poor ground clearance and a hunched-up driving position. These faults were never eradicated, and just how rushed the design was is demonstrated by the large number of detail modifications in the first two years of production.

Donald Healey and his team were aware of the car's shortcomings and made proposals to counter them, but the sticking point was always BMC and its incompetent bean-counters and marketing people. The Big Healey was seen as a milch cow, bought as a bargain, and throughout its history it suffered from a lack of investment to develop it.

It took some time before the major flaws were acknowledged by road tests, which tended to be fairly sycophantic in the 1950s, but they undoubtedly contributed to the fact that the Healey's production target never came close to being met. Production also remained more or less static, which, in an ever-expanding market, meant that the Healey's initially promising share of the market shrunk over the years.

Early cars, code-named BN1 (BN for 'Body

Launched at the 1955 London Motor Show, the BN2 version of the 100 was basically unchanged externally, but under the surface was a new four-speed gearbox, still with overdrive on the top two gears.

This Coronet Cream car is a 100M, which was a factory-built performance version with a 'Le Mans' engine modification kit and high compression pistons. All 100M models came with a louvred bonnet and securing strap.

Number'), had the Atlantic's four-speed gearbox, but testing showed that the low bottom gear was unnecessary in so light a car and it was blanked off. The resulting three-speed 'box was augmented by an electrically-operated Laycock de Normanville overdrive on the top two ratios, effectively making it an all-synchromesh five-speed 'box. Until November 1961, the gear-shift, modified from a column shift, was on the left-hand side of the transmission tunnel with a cranked gear-lever for right-hand drive cars. The 90bhp at 4000rpm that the all-iron engine developed was unremarkable, but was compensated by 144lb ft torque at 2000rpm. With a kerb weight of 2015lb, the 100 could cover 0-60mph in 10.3sec and reach 103mph.

When quoting performance figures, unless otherwise indicated, I have taken them from *The Autocar* because it used a fifth wheel to obtain its figures. Other road testers of equal integrity did not have that benefit, and in the 1950s there were plenty of journalists whose standards were a disgrace. In the main they were employed in Fleet Street and their idea of blistering criticism was fearlessly to draw attention to the position of the ash-tray while glossing over the fact that a car had no performance, handling or brakes.

Even the best road testers, however, were in the hands of manufacturers. Individual cars could show remarkable variances since manufacturing standards were not consistent and the way a car had been run-in could make a big difference. Some manufacturers even prepared special cars for road tests (BMC was rumbled by *Motor Sport* magazine in the early 1950s and later the original Jaguar E-type was a notorious example) and it is possible that some early Healeys released for test had tuned engines and aluminium panels. Some makers recalibrated instruments to obtain better performance figures, a scam which was able to fool some of the less efficient, or less well-equipped, road testers. It is a fact that some performance figures for the BN1 could barely be matched by later works rally cars with twice the power and modifications to eliminate the axle tramp and wind-up which were features of most Healeys.

In common with most sports cars of the day, the Healey's weather equipment consisted of a rudimentary 'stick and fabric' hood and detachable sidescreens, but the windscreen was adjustable and could be folded nearly flat. This was a feature unique to the 100: on earlier sports cars the 'screen could often be folded *forwards*, but on the 100 it could be folded *back* so that air-flow was not disturbed. This facility helped to produce outstanding performance figures for the car, since later models with a fixed windscreen were never able to record such impressive 0-60mph times – but I have already suggested that other factors may have been at play.

In 1954 came the first major variant, the 100S, which was a lightweight competition model. The first important change to the road car, however, was announced at the 1955 London Motor Show when a new four-speed gearbox, with overdrive on the top two ratios, was fitted as standard, and the car's designation became BN2. As BN1 spawned the 100S, so BN2 was also available as the 100M with a tuned engine and a louvred bonnet. BN2 remained in production only for one model year, during which 4604 were made, including a disputed number of 100M versions.

Rationalisation within BMC made it inevitable that the four-cylinder Atlantic engine would have a brief life, and in 1956 came the installation of the six-cylinder 2639cc C-series engine which was used by a number of BMC saloon cars. With the new engine on the horizon, Donald Healey and his team were asked to revise the design in the light of criticisms. A 2in increase in wheelbase and the rearrangement of various other components allowed the inclusion of '+2' seats, although they were really little more than a padded parcel shelf and an intrusion into the already limited boot space. Healey did not like doing this because he felt that it detracted from the car's concept and character – he had other modifications in mind. His view was shared by customers, who began to perceive the Healey as a fast tourer rather than an out-and-out sports car. Worse, few thought that the new engine was an improvement.

The 100-Six (BN4) of 1956 was distinguished by an oval grille with wrinkled horizontal bars, an Austin styling feature of the time. Its windscreen was no longer adjustable, pressed steel wheels became standard (most buyers preferred the added-cost optional wires) and a heater and overdrive became extras. The brilliant bargain which was the 100 began to be a little tarnished as the basic price (in Britain) rose modestly from £750 to £762, but items which had been standard on the 100 added £139 10s to the price of the 100-Six.

The first important variation of the 100 theme came in 1954 with the 100S, a lightweight competition model – five special works cars and 50 production versions were built. Visible changes from this angle include a racing windscreen and a quick-release fuel filler.

A new oval grille with wrinkled bars, an Austin styling feature of the time, was a distinguishing point of the 100-Six, seen here in new 2+2 form and with an optional hardtop. Under the bonnet was a BMC C-series six-cylinder engine of 2639cc.

Despite an increase in power to 102bhp at 4600rpm, the 100-Six was less lively than the 100: while its top speed remained 103mph, the 0-60mph leg slowed from 10.3sec to 12.9sec. Few people would call this progress, but it may partly be explained by the fact that the fixed windscreen increased drag while the new engine, interior refinements and longer wheelbase added 320lb. Front/rear weight distribution, which had been 50/50, became 49/51, and some drivers claimed that it affected the Healey's sharp handling.

During 1957, Healey production moved from Longbridge to the MG works at Abingdon, so production was suspended for a while. This was not unwelcome for BMC since the 100-Six had not been well-received in the USA and the break in production allowed the stock-pile to dwindle. When production resumed there were revisions to the engine which transformed it and the car. Power increased to 117bhp at 4750rpm and maximum torque moved slightly up the rev range, improvements which increased top speed to 111mph and reduced 0-60mph to 11.2sec, which was still shy of the original 100's time.

For those who could do without the '+2' seating, the two-seat BN6 became an option in mid-1958 and

17

Visually unchanged from the 100-Six, the 3000 MkI was powered by a larger six-cylinder engine of 2912cc, power rising from 117bhp to 124bhp. Two-tone colour schemes – this is Healey Blue over Ivory White – suit the Healey's lines particularly well.

4150 were built. The fact that BMC made a two-seat sports car, replaced it with a 2+2 with less performance, got the engine right and then made a two-seater as an option, says everything you need to know about the corporation.

There was a time when manufacturers kept the wraps on new models until their national motor show, and never indulged in today's carefully-contrived leaks and 'scoop' photographs. Since most Big Healeys went to the US, however, it was at the New York Motor Show in March 1959 that the Austin-Healey 3000 made its debut. BMC enlarged the C-series engine to 2912cc by increasing the bore within a new block casting, which became standard on all cars with C-series engines. As fitted to the 3000, it gave 124bhp at 4600rpm, top speed went up to 114mph (when fitted with the optional hardtop which improved the aerodynamics) and the 0-60mph dash improved to

11.4sec, which was still a long way short of the dubious figures for the original 100.

Two-seat (BN7) and 2+2 (BT7) versions of the 3000 were offered and each had disc brakes on the front wheels. In a two-year production life, 10,825 BT7s were made while the popularity of the two-seat option declined, with just 2825 BN7s made. The Healey was clearly perceived as a sports-tourer rather than as a serious sports car.

The 3000 MkII arrived in 1961 with a restyled grille and triple SU carburettors. Power went up to 132bhp at 4750rpm and there was a small increase in torque, but it proved difficult to keep the carburettors in tune and twin carbs were fitted a year later with hardly any difference. As before, one could have a two-seater (BN7) or 2+2 (BT7), but most buyers continued to choose the latter – only 355 BN7s were sold to 5095 BT7s. As the Healey was increasingly seen as a tourer, its boot space, which was considered outstanding in 1952, now received criticism, as did cockpit heat, engine noise and pedal layout. Top speed on the MkII was 112mph (BT7) and the 0-60mph time, on which so much emphasis is placed these days, was 11.5sec.

The 3000 MkII arrived in 1961 with another power increase, to 132bhp, thanks to the use of tricky-to-tune triple SU carburettors. The new grille with vertical bars is an instant identification feature.

Late in its life, from 1964, the Healey moved into 3000 MkIII guise, with 150bhp and substantial revisions to make the interior more comfortable. This striking, but original, colour is Metallic Golden Beige.

With the MkII Convertible of 1962 (BJ7), the Healey improved significantly in practicality. There was a permanently-fixed foldaway hood, a curved windscreen with quarterlights, winding windows and chromework on top of the doors. There was no pretence that the car was other than a tourer and the two-seat option was dropped The troublesome triple SUs were discarded in favour of a twin-carb system for little loss of power or torque, and road testers actually reported a higher top speed (117mph) and improved acceleration (0-60mph in 10.4 sec), which may have been due to the curved windscreen improving the aerodynamics.

The spring of 1964 brought the 3000 MkIII (BJ8) and the last revisions to the design. Engine power was increased to 148bhp, which translated into a top speed of 121mph and 0-60mph in 9.8sec. During 1964 (the moment is a matter of debate) came the 'Phase II' model, which had chassis modifications to allow more suspension travel while the Panhard rod locating the rear axle was replaced by radius arms.

Although the Big Healey was dated, these changes had a positive effect on production and 1966 saw the best sales (5494) since 1960 (7005). A total of 16,322

'Phase II' Healeys were made, making it the most popular variant of the car. It was also the best and, today, the most desirable production 3000, even if it had fallen behind its rivals – it was still in production when Lotus was marketing the mid-engined Europa and the third version of the Elan.

American safety and emission laws, the first of which came into force on 1 January 1968, were given as the reason for ending production in December 1967 (one car was assembled in 1968). It was judged uneconomic to modify the design to meet the changes and besides BMH (as BMC had become) had more pressing problems. By the end of 1968 it would be part of British Leyland and would enter an even more troubled stage as decades of mismanagement came together to implode.

Donald Healey proposed a solution by building the Austin-Healey 4000 powered by the 4-litre six-cylinder engine which Rolls-Royce supplied for the Vanden Plas Princess R saloon. Even in standard form this engine produced 175bhp and there was more to come with tuning. But the proposal was rejected and thus began the steady decline of the mass-produced British sports car.

19

AUSTIN-HEALEY 100

After the war America began its love affair with the British sports car. Domestic products offered superb value for money but a section of young America preferred to lay out more for an MG which provided markedly less performance than, say, a Ford Coupe yet was more fun to drive. MG created the bridgehead and was soon followed by Jaguar with the XK120, then the Healey, followed by the Triumph TR2 and the AC Ace.

Britain was the only European country which made sports cars in significant numbers since most others struggled to make cars of any description. French companies that had made so many outstanding sports cars in the 1920s and 1930s were hit by fiscal measures designed to encourage motoring for the masses, and one by one they folded. The 1950s belonged to the British sports car.

When the Austin-Healey 100 began production in 1953, it occupied a place in the market between Jaguar and MG. Sunbeam-Talbot introduced the original Alpine later that year, but it was overweight, underpowered and expensive – it did not last long and nor did it deserve to. Soon after the 100 went into production Triumph began to make the TR2, which was close to the Healey in performance yet undercut it in price. Once the TR2 came on stream, the Healey could no longer boast that it was the world's cheapest 100mph car.

In mid-1953 the mass-produced sports car market looked like this:

	Top speed	0-60mph	Price
Austin-Healey 100	103mph	10.3sec	$3000
Chevrolet Corvette	110mph	11.0sec	$3400
Jaguar XK120	120mph	10.0sec	$3345
MG TF	85mph	20.0sec	$2200
Nash-Healey	105mph	13.0sec	$6200
Porsche 356 'Super'	95mph	12.5sec	$4200
Triumph TR2	103mph	11.9sec	$2400

True to Leonard Lord's intention, in Britain the Healey was a basic £750 plus purchase tax of £313 12s 6d, although that was largely academic since few cars were allocated to the home market. Looking at the choice for American customers, one notes that the Jaguar XK120 was only 10% more expensive than the 100, which may help to explain why the Healey's production target of 200 cars a week was never attained. In fact, the most authoritative estimate of BN1 output (1953-55) was 10,030 and of BN2 (1955-56) was 4604.

Of course, one cannot go on performance figures and price alone when assessing the appeal of sports cars. Leaving aside the Nash-Healey, which was an aberration, the Porsche 356 looks the least good buy – at the time it was still using a tuned VW Beetle engine – yet Porsche went from strength to strength because it had a special, indefinable ingredient which appealed to drivers. One can understand why the Chevrolet Corvette sold slowly in its early years (it would have been axed had Ford not introduced the Thunderbird) because it had an antiquated engine, two-speed Powerglide automatic transmission and problems with its fibreglass body – and Chevrolet had no glamour.

By contrast, the market was ripe for the Austin-Healey 100. While its sales figures were disappointing, it did not disappoint its drivers. True, the driving position recalled vintage motoring and heat from the engine made the cockpit uncomfortably warm. True, the low-slung exhaust system could give problems with ground clearance and many an exhaust was knocked off, but the car was capable of reaching the magic 'ton' and would turn heads in any company. People even thought that the luggage space was generous but then there were still sports cars in production with no separate boot.

While the first 20 cars were panelled in aluminium, production models had pressed steel bodies, although there were aluminium panels around the bonnet and

Sitting in an early production version of his new sports car, Donald Healey shakes hands with BMC Chief Executive Leonard Lord in February 1953. The tie-up between Austin and Healey had been agreed at the Earls Court Motor Show four months earlier.

The Autocar's September 1953 road test car, with windscreen folded and tonneau cover in place. Unlike the prototype, production 100s had wire wheels as standard – but these 48-spoke Dunlop wheels had a weakness for snapping spokes on cars that were driven hard.

boot, an arrangement which was to lead to corrosion problems later. Some early cars in the production run also had aluminium bonnets and boots. The bonnet itself was hinged at the front and the boot had a pair of chromed exterior hinges which were longer than they strictly needed to be, but which created the effect of twin flashes.

Chromework was used sparingly but effectively. This was unusual at a time when chrome was being larded onto cars, although a chromed strip on top of the scuttle was disliked because it reflected light into

the driver's eyes. Contemporary fashion was catered for by a range of two-tone colour schemes, and no car has every carried a two-tone scheme with greater elegance. Until August 1953 the boot bore the legend 'Austin of England' in flowing script but thereafter it was changed to 'Austin-Healey' in a style to match the bonnet badge. This seems to indicate that BMC was not quite sure how to present the car – which was typical of its marketing.

To gain access to the cockpit, one reached over the doors and pulled back a knob – there were no

Although it was a severely flawed car put into production without sufficient development, the Healey's pure lines were beyond criticism.

The large grille was a feature of all the four-cylinder cars, but this quintessential colour, Healey Blue, remained available until the end of 3000 MkIII production in 1967.

external handles and the car could not be locked. Pull-cords inside the doors opened them when getting out. Two bucket seats with Dunlopillo cushioning were upholstered mainly in leather, with Vynide used for sections, such as the backs, which would not suffer wear. These were considered extremely good seats at the time, but were criticised for lack of lateral support by 1960. Early cars had an awkward peg adjustment system (on the driver's seat only) and a sliding system was not employed until December 1953, at which point the original adjustable steering column was replaced with a fixed column. The cockpit was carpeted and there was a detachable central armrest on top of the transmission tunnel.

A heater was usually fitted as standard (but omitted on cars delivered to tropical markets) and was augmented by engine heat which permeated the footwells. It was given out at the time that bulkhead sound and heat insulation was deliberately skimpy to keep the car's weight down, but it was more a case of keeping down the price and rushing the prototype into production without dealing with the problem. To counteract the additional heat, there was an air vent under the right-hand side of the dashboard, and the real fresh air enthusiast could fold back the windscreen.

A parcel shelf was mounted under the dashboard on the passenger's side, while the hollow doors

The long-stroke, slow-revving, four-cylinder 2660cc engine, breathing through twin SU carburettors, produced 90bhp at 4000rpm and a respectable 144lb ft of torque at 2000rpm.

An ingenious mechanism allows the 100's windscreen to be folded, although in practice it's as well to don goggles and flying helmet before attempting to drive at speed in this configuration.

provided more storage space. This was welcome since the boot was not very capacious and became even less so when a customer specified the optional larger fuel tank. The spare wheel, lying flat in the boot, protruded into the space behind the seats where the hood, hood sticks, full-width tonneau cover (with central zip) and detachable sidescreens were stored. Two 6-volt batteries were mounted under the floor in front of the rear axle, and the filler cap was inside the boot on all four-cylinder 100 variants except the 100S.

Facing the driver was a painted metal dashboard which held, left to right, a combined oil pressure/water temperature gauge, speedometer with tripmeter, rev counter and fuel gauge. The overdrive switch was

The installation of the Austin A70/90 gearbox was thoroughly unconventional on the BN1. The linkage came through the side of the tunnel and bottom gear was blanked off, giving only three speeds – although standard overdrive made this a five-speed 'box in practice.

The badge on the boot lid typified Austin's initial uncertainty about how to market the 100: this 'Austin of England' script was used until August 1953, then replaced by the legend 'Austin-Healey'.

also on the dash. A mirror was mounted on the middle of the scuttle, but rearward visibility was tricky with the hood in place. The gearchange was mounted on the floor to the left of the transmission tunnel (it began life as a column change on the Austin A70) and was cranked towards the driver on right-hand drive models, while a 'fly-off' handbrake was mounted to the right of the tunnel.

A 16½in Bluemels steering wheel incorporated a horn and self-cancelling indicator switch. Originally the cam and peg steering gear (ex-Austin A70 and A90) was made by Burman, but from March 1956 a new box made by Cam Gears was specified. Regardless of the mechanism used, the steering was relatively high-geared on the 100. With a ratio of 12.6:1 (it would change on later models), it took roughly 2½ turns lock-to-lock and the turning circle was 35ft. Most road testers, however, agreed that the steering was unusually precise – a view still expressed by modern drivers.

Like all previous Healeys, the chassis was of box section construction. Healey production had begun in 1946 in the workshop of a Humber distributor called Westlands in which there was a metal folder capable of folding sheet steel up to 8ft in length – and so 8ft became a design parameter. The main chassis rails, which were parallel members, were boxes 3½in deep and 3in wide, placed 17in apart and braced by a dual crossmember at the front, a boxed cruciform structure a little aft of middle, and another crossmember at the rear. Built from a number of metal pressings welded together, the bulkhead/scuttle was welded to the chassis, as were the main body members, in order to reduce scuttle shake. The Healey was good in this

department for a 1952 car, but scuttle shake was never completely eliminated.

The three-bearing pushrod engine came from the Austin Atlantic, but it could trace its origins to the famous 1928 Chevrolet 'Stove-Bolt' Six. When General Motors bought Bedford, the British commercial vehicle manufacturer, the engine was used in Bedford trucks, and when Austin began making trucks in 1938 it unashamedly copied the Bedford/Chevrolet unit, a direct derivative of which powered the first Corvettes. During the war Austin was asked to make a four-cylinder engine for a military vehicle and it lopped two cylinders from the straight-six. In 2199cc form this engine appeared in the 1945 Austin 16 saloon and subsequently in the A70 Hampshire and the Austin taxi.

The engine was bored out to 2660cc (87.3mm × 111.1mm) for the A90 Atlantic and produced 90bhp at 4000rpm with a compression ratio of 7.5:1 (the quality of available fuel limited compression ratios) and twin 1½in SU H4 carburettors. Like most long-stroke engines of the time, it revved slowly but purposefully to its 4800rpm maximum, and produced a respectable 144lb ft of torque at 2000rpm.

With muscle like this in a relatively light car, the low bottom gear in the four-speed A70/90 gearbox was redundant and it was blanked off, creating an unconventional gear-shift pattern. A Laycock de Normanville electrically-actuated overdrive operating on the top two gears was fitted as standard, effectively giving the Healey a five-speed transmission with synchromesh on all gears. As customers had the option of a lower rear axle ratio, so too a lower overdrive ratio was an option.

In North America, which took the majority of production in the early years, Austin advertised the Healey with "another sleek beauty", a Republic F-84F Thunderstreak.

The coil spring and wishbone front suspension came from the Atlantic and A70 Hereford saloon. An anti-roll bar attached to the lower wishbones and Armstrong lever-arm shock absorbers acted on the upper wishbones. Throughout the Healey's life only minor modifications were made to this system; the shock absorbers were stiffened after six months, for example, and slightly longer springs were used later.

Much the same production continuity is true of the rear suspension, which had semi-elliptical springs, Armstrong lever-arm shock absorbers and a Panhard rod which ran between brackets on the right-hand chassis member and the left-hand spring bolts. The Panhard rod was insufficient to prevent axle tramp and

'wind-up' on initial take-off, although excellent performance figures, curiously, were still obtained by magazines. In the first year of production three different types of springs were used: the earliest cars used two patterns of seven-leaf springs, but in February 1954 eight-leaf springs were fitted in response to complaints about exhaust pipes being knocked off over rough surfaces, and these remained standard until the 3000 MkIII 'Phase II' of 1964.

At first the live rear axle was the spiral bevel type used on the A70 and A90, but from November 1954 a (heavier) hypoid axle with a slightly higher final drive

There's nothing to distinguish it externally, but this Spruce Green car is a BN2, the four-speed derivative introduced in 1955 and produced only for one year. Since only 4604 BN2s were built, this is now one of the most desirable Healey models.

The interior was reasonably lavish for a sports car, with excellent bucket seats, carpet in the footwells, a padded armrest on the centre tunnel, comprehensive instrumentation and a heater fitted as standard.

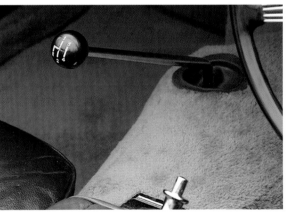

The well-equipped instrument panel and standard Bluemels three-spoke steering wheel of the 100 model, seen here on a BN2. The switch on the hub of the steering wheel operates the direction indicators.

Although the gear lever on the BN2 was still offset, it now emerged from the top of the tunnel and gave the driver a choice of four gears, two with overdrive.

Any Austin-Healey 100 could be uprated to 100bhp with the bolt-on 'Le Mans' engine kit (which included larger carburettors, a special inlet manifold and a carburettor cold air box), but the factory-built 100M model added high compression pistons to take power up to 110bhp.

The 100M, of which 640 were built by the factory, was an improved BN2 fitted with a 'Le Mans' tuning kit, louvred bonnet and leather bonnet strap.

ratio (4.1:1 instead of 4.125:1) was fitted, although a lower ratio (3.667:1) remained a customer option. The rear axle's location above the main chassis members restricted suspension movement until the MkIII 'Phase II', on which kinks in the chassis members allowed extra movement.

While the prototype Healey Hundred had 10in Girling drum brakes, 11in Girlings were specified for production and the front brakes had two leading shoes. When the hypoid rear axle was introduced, 2¼in width rear drums replaced the original 1⅜in width drums – until then Alfin drums had been an optional extra.

Dunlop 48-spoke 4J-15 wire wheels with chromed knock–off hubs were fitted as standard, against the general trend to use stiffer pressed steel wheels. While they fulfilled their function of enhancing the Healey's looks, the wire wheels had a tendency to snap their spokes when the car was driven even moderately hard and modifications to the wheel design introduced in August 1954 did not eliminate this weakness. DHM knew there was a problem, but BMC had agreed a long–term supply contract with Dunlop and was stuck with 48-spoke wheels until the contract had been completed.

From August 1955 a four-speed gearbox, courtesy

Miss Great Britain of 1955 participated in publicity photography of the revised BN2 model. The windscreen is in the streamlined position, but the press release accompanying this shot avoided discussion of frontal areas.

of the new Austin A90 Westminster, was fitted as standard and cars with this were code-named BN2. There was no synchromesh on bottom gear, but the gear-shift pattern became conventional. Since overdrive was retained on the top two gears, BN2 had a six-speed transmission. The clutch housing was separate on BN2 (it was incorporated into the gearbox casing on BN1), but the same Borg & Beck 9in single dry-plate unit was used.

It is a great pity, but there is no point in quoting from contemporary road tests to see how the car measured up to its rivals in specific areas because road testing was not as analytical as it is today. When the Healey appeared in 1953, there had been precious few new designs for 14 years and the simple fact that it had an 'all-enveloping' body was enough to win approval. It was a thoroughly modern car, a foretaste of delights to come. It was like giving a starving man a loaf of white bread – he is not likely to say he prefers brown.

In retrospect we may judge the Healey as having too harsh a ride, of needing muscle to steer it, of having a hot cockpit, a noisy and vulnerable exhaust and a cramped driving position, but at the time these were more or less normal.

Road testers were thrilled by the performance, commented on how good the brakes were, and

reported that the car offered a surprisingly roomy cockpit and pleasantly easy access through the wide doors. Observations about handling were restricted to a few brief remarks about it having natural understeer with oversteer on demand. Much emphasis, however, was placed on the fact that the Healey could be driven fast without it wandering all over the road, which says something about other sports cars on the market.

The Healey's firm suspension was praised at first, and only later did testers complain that the car was thrown off-course by bumps in the road – which suggests that the Healey did not keep pace with developments. The fact that the hood was weatherproof was another point in its favour – and another sideways comment on rival cars. Little was made of the fact that the Healey had 14 greasing points needing attention every 500 miles, because this was not uncommon.

It is hard now to imagine the impact that the Healey had with its sinuous, ageless lines and 100mph performance. The Healey's appeal was mainly visual, and to criticise it was like being offered a date with Ingrid Bergman and demurring on the grounds that she might not cook a good breakfast.

A BN1 with rudimentary hood erected and detachable sidescreens (complete with lower flap for hand signals) in place. The man at the wheel is S.C.H. 'Sammy' Davis, long-time Sports Editor of *The Autocar*.

The 100M

In 1953 Austin-Healey entered two lightly modified cars at Le Mans driven by competent amateurs. They achieved 119mph on the Mulsanne Straight and 12th and 14th overall. It was a superb performance for a relatively unaltered mass-produced sports car and one which led Healey to appropriate the name 'Le Mans' for a bolt-on tuning kit which was available from any dealer. The 100M, however, had this tuning kit as standard equipment – and a little more besides.

The 'Le Mans' Modification Kit consisted of a pair of 1¾in HD6 SU carburettors mounted on a special manifold, a carburettor cold air box, high-lift camshaft, stronger valve springs, a steel-faced cylinder head gasket and a distributor with a special advance curve. On the carburettor cold air box was a brass plate proclaiming "This car has been fitted with a 'Le Mans' Modification Kit".

Any Austin-Healey 100 could be fitted with the kit, which would increase engine power to 100bhp at 4500rpm. The 100M, however, was a factory-built BN2 with a stiffer anti-roll bar, the 'Le Mans' kit and high-compression (8.1:1) pistons giving 110bhp. Performance improved to a top speed of 109mph and 0-60mph in 9.6sec without losing any of the Healey's flexibility or instant response.

Externally, the main feature of the 100M was a louvred bonnet with a leather strap across it. Despite what has been written elsewhere, two-tone paintwork was not standard – but about 70% of owners specified it. The factory appears to have built 640 100Ms, while a further 519 (a number which included some BN1s) were modified by the Healey works at Warwick.

It was also possible to buy other accessories, including aero-screens, a 'racing' silencer, alternative final drive ratios, larger fuel tanks and the distinctive louvred bonnet (for £15 10s). Some standard cars with the louvred bonnet passed themselves off in the street as 100Ms, while cars which were fitted with the conversion kit did not necessarily have the bonnet.

No Big Healey was particularly successful in motor racing at a serious level and the 100M was no exception. On the other hand, the modifications turned the basic 100 into a better road car, while the louvred bonnet and leather strap added a touch of distinction without compromising the aesthetics.

The 100S

The 100S (code-named 'AHS'), the first independent project undertaken by the Donald Healey Motor Company after it had allied with BMC, took shape during 1953 and 1954. Although it was an official Austin-Healey model, the chassis plate simply bore the name 'Healey' because the five special cars (some

The regular '100' flash on the radiator grille gained the appropriate suffix letter on the 100M model.

Cars fitted with the 'Le Mans' kit had an identifying brass plate on the carburettor cold air box.

There's no doubting the competition intentions of the 100S. Stripped-down in appearance, it has a perspex windscreen without wipers, a smaller radiator grille, a louvred bonnet and no bumpers.

authorities say there were eight) used by the works, and the 50 production cars, were all developed and built at Warwick.

At first the model was called the Special Test Car, a term which covered anything (including, one suspects, specially-prepared road test cars), partly because BMC's attitude to competition was ambivalent – which is a polite way of saying that BMC had no coherent policy at all. The foundation for the Special Test Cars was laid with the modified

100s which had run at Le Mans in 1953, but pukka Special Test Cars appeared early in 1954, with Dunlop magnesium alloy centre-lock wheels and a David Brown (Aston Martin) four-speed gearbox. Although the earliest cars were panelled in aluminium, the body was initially standard Healey in shape – the distinctive tilted nose with its smaller grille evolved during development. After a Special Test Car finished third in the 1954 Sebring 12-Hour race, the name was changed to 100S (for Sebring).

DHM entered cars in selected events during 1954, and the 100S was unveiled as a production car at the 1954 London Motor Show, although none was delivered until the following February.

Externally the production 100S was distinguished

Although the 100S's chassis structure was unchanged, the use of aluminium body panels and other weight-saving measures helped to reduce dry weight from 2015lb to 1700lb.

Not much space for luggage: the boot of the 100S was occupied by a 20-gallon fuel tank connected by a wide-bore pipe to a racing-type filler.

These seats were unique to the 100S. Were they intended to cool down overheating occupants or simply to save a little more weight?

Compared with a normal Healey four-cylinder unit, the cylinder head is aluminium instead of cast-iron and the larger carburettors of the 100S are mounted on the other side of the engine. Maximum power was 132bhp at 4700rpm.

by a louvred bonnet and leather strap, an absence of bumpers, a low perspex windscreen with no wipers, and a small oval grille. Other detail changes were two chromed metal clips holding the trailing edge of the bonnet, a quick-release filler cap mounted externally above the right-hand side of the boot, 5.50-15 Dunlop racing tyres and twin exhaust pipes peeking under the right-hand door. Weather equipment was not provided and trim in the cockpit was stripped to a bare minimum.

Because the 100S was primarily a competition car, all were made with right-hand drive since most circuits traditionally run clockwise and therefore have more right-hand corners than left-handers. The seats had vertical slats cut into them for ventilation and a driver's lap belt was fitted to comply with the regulations of the Sports Car Club of America.

Although the chassis and internal body assemblies were standard Austin-Healey, the body panels were in aluminium, which, with other detail weight saving measures, reduced dry weight from 2015lb to 1700lb. Just as there is some doubt about the integrity of the performance figures for the standard car, so there are discrepancies in quoted weight figures, which leads one to wonder whether some road test cars were fitted with aluminium panels. Much of the boot space was occupied by a 20-gallon fuel tank with the spare wheel strapped to the top and accessible from inside the cockpit by tipping the passenger seat forward. Since the battery was located in the left-hand footwell, a passenger was definitely an after-thought.

Harry Weslake, the gas-flow specialist, developed an aluminium cylinder head with individual porting. Reversing the normal layout, the carburettors and manifolds were on the right-hand side, with the spark plugs and other electrical ancillaries on the left. Items from the 'Le Mans' Modification Kit were incorporated, together with solid-skirt pistons giving a compression ratio of 8.3:1 and a crankshaft of hardened Nitralloy. The twin SU carburettors were served by twin fuel pumps, and a new steel flywheel, competition clutch and finned alloy oil cooler were added. The result was an engine which developed 132bhp at 4700rpm and 168lb ft torque at 2500rpm.

Works cars usually ran with a David Brown four-speed gearbox and Dunlop magnesium alloy disc wheels with central-lock hubs. For the works cars' last major race, the 1956 Sebring 12-Hours, two twin-choke Webers, revised cam profiles and a new fabricated exhaust system were fitted to the two entries. These modifications raised output to 145bhp, but in the race the exhaust systems broke and caused the retirement of both cars.

Production cars had a BMC four-speed gearbox of the type fitted to the BN2, but with close-ratio gears and no overdrive. A spiral bevel rear axle was fitted and customers had the choice of four final drive ratios. There were stiffer (Armstrong RXP) shock absorbers, special high-power Lucas headlights and uprated electrical ancillaries such as the works had used at Le Mans, a wood-rimmed steering wheel and an adjustable steering column.

Perhaps the most startling modification was the use of Dunlop disc brakes all round, allowing the 100S a claim to be the first production sports car to have discs on all four wheels. The Jaguar D-type (of which more were made) also had four-wheel discs and, like the 100S, was launched as a production car at the 1954 London Motor Show. The prototype Healey raced before the first D-type, but the first production D-type

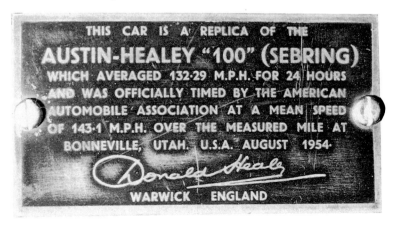

This dashboard plaque was fitted to production versions of the 100S and explains all. Don't be misled by today's normal automotive use of the word 'replica': this car is the genuine article and the most sought-after of all Healeys.

The 100S cabin has an even more sporting appearance, with simpler seats and a special steering wheel with aluminium spokes and a wooden rim.

was delivered before the first production 100S. The term 'production sports car' is emphasised, however, because Chrysler offered four-wheel disc brakes on a saloon in 1949, but soon reverted to drum brakes. Those are the facts, now debate.

Production of the 100S began in February 1955 and the run lasted until November. The Warwick factory was geared up to build 20 cars a month but once again the target was not reached, largely because the 100S disappointed in competition. Exactly half of the 50 production versions went to the USA with the rest distributed around the world.

On each car was a plaque which boasted that a prototype had averaged 132.29mph for 24 hours on the Salt Lake Flats in Utah and had recorded a mean speed of 143.1mph over the measured mile. These are impressive figures, but record attempts in the 1950s often produced freak results and one reason was fuel. High-grade fuel was not universally available, so manufacturers were conservative with compression ratios. Organising a record attempt, however, was a different matter and an engine could be tweaked to make use of the best available fuel. Other standard modifications for record runs were tonneaus and aero-screens, while the Bonneville flats provided so much space that very high final drive ratios could be fitted.

In fact, top speed of the production 100S was

126mph with 0-60mph covered in 7.8sec – according to *Road & Track*. John Bolster, testing a 100S for *Autosport,* attained only 121.6mph and 0-60mph in 9.8sec, although his car was fitted with a regular 100 windscreen which must have acted as an air-brake. The 1955 Chevrolet Corvette with a 4343cc V8 was good for 119mph/8.7sec while the 1955 3.4-litre Jaguar XK140 returned 129mph/9.2sec but the 100S cost less than the Jaguar. If you could get your hands on a 100S in Britain (eight were sold on the home market), it cost £1250 inclusive of tax.

Viewed as a competent dual-purpose road and competition car, the 100S was a bargain. But it was out of its depth in international racing, save in those events which permitted it to run as a production sports car – and there were few of those. In sprint racing the 100S could not match 2-litre cars like the AC Ace-Bristol or any Frazer Nash. It is true that these hand-built rivals were much more expensive than the Healey, but they remained the opposition and the 100S could not match their nimble handling.

At £1250, however, the 100S provided good value for a keen amateur who had a sensible car for weekdays, yet could drive it to a circuit, paint on numbers, and have a good time while not expecting to win. The trouble was that DHM had grander intentions when it created the 100S.

THE HEALEY IN RACING

To put it bluntly, the Healey was not a great racing car and the ambitions of the Donald Healey Motor Company far out-weighed its achievements. Its few successes tended to be class wins, which was not difficult because when it appeared in 1953, and for several years after, there were no other production 3-litre sports cars…

Indeed, since there were no mass-produced sports cars apart from Austin-Healey, MG, Triumph and Jaguar, which were in different capacity classes, production sports car racing was not common in Britain in the early 1950s – and when it occurred it was usually on a handicap basis. Instead the Healey often competed against specialist machines, usually with 2-litre Bristol engines, built in tiny numbers by makers such as Cooper, Lister, Tojeiro and Frazer Nash, against which the Healey stood little chance. It was only in the strictly amateur races organised by the

Sports Car Club of America that Austin-Healey achieved success. It dominated Class D Production and was overall national champion in 1954, but there was virtually nothing else in its class.

Austin-Healey's greatest competition successes would come in rallying, but not until the 3000 of 1959. A works 100S ran in the 1955 Liège-Sofia-Liège Rally, but crashed soon after the start, and the exercise was not repeated for some time. Until the late 1950s BMC was less committed to rallying than most of its rivals, and tended to enter models it wished to promote, the Austin Westminster for example, rather than cars which were more suitable. By contrast, when Triumph made the TR2 it reduced the donor engine from 2088cc to 1991cc so that it could compete as a 2-litre car, and the policy paid dividends. When Triumph TR2s took 1-2 in the 1954 RAC Rally, all the Healey could boast were a few wins in SCCA

In the Healey's first season of competition, 1953, a pair of cars ran at Le Mans, finishing 12th and 14th in an impressive display of reliability. This is the 14th-placed car of Maurice Becquart and Gordon Wilkins.

An Ulster amateur, C.B. Carter, demonstrates the Healey's forgiving handling during the 50-mile Munster race at Cork in 1954.

Probably the Healey's finest hour in motor racing: George Abecassis finished 11th overall in a field of over 500 starters for the 1955 Mille Miglia.

racing and 5-lap handicap events in Britain.

In racing at international level, the 100, and its derivatives, competed against out-and-out racers made by the likes of Aston Martin, Ferrari, Gordini, Jaguar, Lancia, Maserati and Mercedes-Benz. As if that was not handicap enough, its slow-revving engine was not ideal for racing *and* it competed in the 3-litre class with a 2.6-litre engine.

Three Healeys ran in the 1953 Mille Miglia, but retired with throttle and clutch problems. At Le Mans the two works cars were essentially standard save for aero-screens, a tonneau over the passenger seat, an uprated electrical system and some aluminium panels – they appear to have come from the prototype batch built by Tickford. The engines were tuned and the

modifications became the basis for the 'Le Mans' modification kit (see the 100M section).

It is often written that Healeys finished 12th and 14th and second and third in class at Le Mans in 1953, but it is less often noted that there were only six cars in the class and three of those retired. It was, however, an impressive reliability run for a production sports car. One also reads that an Austin-Healey finished 11th in the Goodwood 9-Hours, but one does not tend to read that the race was really a glorified British club event.

Donald Healey and his crew at Warwick began work on a competition version which would enter limited production as the 100S. A works development version ran in the 1954 Sebring 12-Hours and finished

Celebrating one of the better 100S racing performances, sixth overall and class victory at Sebring in 1955, are (from left) Donald Healey, Stirling Moss and Lance Macklin.

The 100S in racing action nearer home, Dick Protheroe at the wheel during a Mallory Park 'clubbie' in 1955.

third overall and second in class. It sounds an impressive result since Sebring was a round of the World Sports Car Championship, and some have been quick to say that it might have been a win save for a broken rocker arm late in the race, but then the works Lancias would have been 1-2-3 had they survived. Apart from Austin-Healey, only six other works cars were entered and five of those retired. The race was won by a privately-owned 1500cc Osca, which puts a different perspective on the result.

In the 1954 Mille Miglia, the works 100Ss were transferred from the Gran Turismo class to the large sports car class because no catalogue was submitted to prove they were genuine production cars – and nor were they. Lance Macklin, a very talented driver who embraced motor racing as part of a raffish life style, was 23rd overall and fifth in class behind pukka sports-racers, but a 2-litre Fiat 8V came ninth overall.

It was possibly his treatment at the Mille Miglia which caused Donald Healey to withdraw from Le Mans and to issue a statement protesting against the type of car permitted to run in what, he said, was

supposed to be a race primarily for *bona fide* production car makers. Healey had a point since the organisers at Le Mans had previously tightened the regulations, forcing Cunningham to build road cars to comply with them, but sports car racing was in a state of flux and specials were being allowed to run. Healey spoiled his case when he claimed that 'single-seater' sports cars were being allowed to race, whereas all that had happened was that the organisers of the Mille Miglia had allowed drivers to run without a passenger. Nevertheless, Healey had a valid point: the rules said that prototypes of cars intended for production were eligible (the Jaguar D-type was a case in point), but many entries were thinly disguised racing cars. At a time when you were not supposed to cry 'foul!', Healey's action looked like sour grapes and received an unfavourable reception from press and public alike.

In 1955 several major sports car events incorporated new class systems which encouraged production sports cars, and by this time the 100S qualified as a production car. A 100S was driven by Stirling Moss and Lance Macklin to sixth overall at

Into the six-cylinder period, a factory-built 3000 MkI raced at Le Mans in 1960, but Jack Sears and Peter Riley retired in the ninth hour with a broken con rod.

A contrasting pair of Healeys in historic racing action in 1991, with John Chatham at the wheel of his famous DD 300. This 3000 MkI, the very car raced by Sears/Riley at Le Mans in 1960 (above) but subsequently re-registered, has been campaigned continuously by Chatham since 1965.

Sebring in 1955, heading a 1-2-3 in a production car class, a better result, qualitatively, than the third place of 1954 since most of the works teams were represented and there was no upper capacity limit. Stirling has written of the 100S: '*Not a bad car, but such a humble engine – mine was only pulling 4400rpm on 5.5×15 tyres at Nassau (later in the year)… and that is hardly the stuff of racing legend.*'

In the Mille Miglia George Abecassis brought his Healey home 11th overall, a superb performance by an unusually brave and experienced driver. This was probably Healey's finest hour – there were over 500 entries for the 1955 Mille Miglia – although it tends not to be highly rated by writers on the marque who

are not motor racing historians. Austin-Healey also took a 1-2 in class, but only in one of the many sub-classes which featured that year – an Isetta bubble car and a Citroën 2CV also won sub-classes.

At Le Mans Lance Macklin was in a 100S which was 'privately-entered' (a diplomatic nicety after Donald Healey's attack the previous year) when he was an innocent party in the worst accident in motor racing history, when Pierre Levegh's Mercedes-Benz was forced off-line, ran up the back of the Healey, flew into the air and exploded in the crowd. Poor Macklin was innocently involved in another fatal accident in the Tourist Trophy at Dundrod, which hastened his retirement from the sport. It was rotten

luck for Austin-Healey to have its top driver eliminated from two of the five major races of the year through no fault of his own or of his car.

In the final race of the 1955 World Sports Car Championship, the Carrera-Panamericana road race, neither team car survived to the end of the second day. Macklin's suffered a misfire on day one and was eliminated for being behind time, while Carroll Shelby lay fourth after the first day but crashed on day two.

Even before the last 100S was made in November 1955, it had been overtaken by the AC Ace-Bristol, which was lighter, had much better handling and braking, and could muster 135bhp when tuned. By 1956 production sports car racing was becoming popular in Britain and in order to make a full grid British organisers frequently used a purely domestic 'up to 2700cc' class which was designed to pit Austin-Healeys against Bristol-engined cars, but even the 100S was out-classed in such company, although John Dalton gave a good account of himself with his 100S.

Works 100S models appeared in only one other major race, the 1956 Sebring 12-Hours, where both cars had new cam profiles, twin two-choke Weber carburettors and special fabricated exhaust manifolds which pushed the engine's output to 145bhp. Both cars retired when the exhaust manifolds fell apart, which was an ignominious end to the car's racing

With aeroscreen fitted, Donald Healey sprints through a measured mile at Bonneville at 142.6mph, at the time the fastest speed ever recorded by a modified mass-produced car.

career. A private 100S was 11th overall and third in a production car class at Sebring, and another was eighth overall in the thinly-supported Reims 12-Hours.

Works 100-Sixes with aerodynamic long noses and triple Weber carburettors ran at Sebring in 1957, but they encountered many problems and only one finished, a fairly lacklustre second in class. In the 1957 Mille Miglia, Tommy Wisdom won the 'Price Class', which was a sub-class for mass-produced sports cars. Austin-Healey won the Manufacturers' Team Prize in the 1958 Sebring 12-Hour race, but again that was a minor achievement. Elsewhere the 100-Six began to make a mark in rallies, but this prologue to the success enjoyed by the 3000 is dealt with later.

When the Sprite entered production in 1958, most of DHM's attention was diverted in its direction, with a great deal of success one might add. As late as 1962, however, an Austin-Healey 3000 ran at Le Mans, but it did not finish.

In New Zealand Ross Jensen (later a works Lister driver) raced a tuned 100 with some success, while a teenaged Bruce McLaren made his name with a phenomenal run of wins in a 100M tuned by his

J.G. Bennett, one of the drivers of the Special Test Cars at Bonneville in 1953, chats with Geoffrey Healey (centre) and A.C. Pilsbury, an American Automobile Association timekeeping official.

At Bonneville in 1956 for Healey's last speed attempts. The car in the foreground is a 100-Six with an extended nose, while the 'streamliner' in the background took Donald Healey (standing on the right in this group) through the flying mile at 203.06mph.

father, but racing in New Zealand was fairly primitive at that time.

Healeys did not make much of a mark in circuit racing save in SCCA events where the class structure was tightly controlled. So when Austin-Healey won the SCCA National Championship in 1957/8/9, it was a case of one car/driver being more dominant in a class than any other car/driver in any other class – which in turn meant that the class was not closely contested. In 1962, for example, Ronnie Bucknum took an Austin-Healey 3000 entered by the Hollywood Sports Car Racing Team to 24 victories from 24 starts. There are two things to note: one is that the car was reputed to develop 200bhp, and the other is that Bucknum, who went on to become Honda's first F1 driver, was in a class of his own.

In Britain, the Healey did not come into its own until the mid-to-late 1960s, and then in Modsports racing. Heavily modified cars, with fibreglass body panels and fat tyres, gave a good account of themselves in the hands of several drivers but notably John Chatham, who was still racing Healeys into the 1990s. There is a slight irony in the fact that Chatham, the most successful European Healey racer, had his most successful period with his Modsports car after production of the Healey ceased in 1967.

In international rallying, however, the position was different. There the Big Healey was to shine, but it would be the 1960s before it made its mark…

Record attempts

Record attempts have lost their popularity and even the Land Speed Record has become a curiosity in latter years, but in the 1950s they were taken very seriously indeed. A successful run was trumpeted as loudly as a win in a major race or rally. It is not hard to see why because they demonstrated reliability as well as speed. You could not take a 100 on a round trip from London to Edinburgh without using a grease gun on it, but long-distance record attempts held out the promise of trouble-free motoring.

A blast along the Jabbeke *autoroute* in Belgium was almost mandatory for a British maker producing a new sports car. Before the prototype appeared at the London Motor Show it had a achieved a two-way run at 106.05mph, which allowed the Healey Hundred to be advertised as the cheapest 100mph car in the world.

A 1956 shakedown on home soil for Healey's streamlined record-breaker, here in its later guise with a supercharged BMC C-series engine. Note the perspex cowl for the driver.

At the end of 1953, a Special Test Car and two standard 100s – selected from a dealer's showroom by a representative of the American Automobile Association – were taken to Bonneville. Each standard car was carefully prepared and fitted with a metal tonneau, a cold air carburettor box and an aero screen (both listed options), and the 3.667:1 optional final drive ratio, while the Special Test Car had a 2.93:1 final drive ratio. Between them they took over 100 records, although most of them were obscure US national records for 3-litre production cars. There were no domestic American 3-litre production cars, and most of the records that the standard Healeys broke had been set by an Austin A90 Atlantic.

The Special Test Car set records up to 12 hours and 3000km, but its engine failed at 18 hours – a fact which was glossed over at the time. Still, it covered the measured mile at 142.6mph, which was the fastest speed then recorded by a modified mass-produced car.

In August 1954, DHM returned to Bonneville with a 100S which completed 24 hours at 132.29mph and covered the flying mile at 143.1mph, feats which were commemorated by a special plaque in each production 100S – as well they might be because these were remarkable runs. Also present at the record run was a 100S with a cast-iron version of the Weslake head, a Shorrock supercharger (which boosted the engine to 224bhp), a five-speed David Brown gearbox

(plus overdrive) and a long-tailed streamlined body. Driven by Donald Healey, it achieved 192.62mph. Between them, the 100S and the 'streamliner' took 52 American National and International 3-litre records.

Healey's last record attempts came in September 1956 to coincide with the launch of the 100-Six. One of the cars was a 100-Six fitted with a long-nose body and a 150bhp engine featuring a high compression six-port cylinder head and triple twin-choke Webers. With customary tweaks such as a very high final drive ratio, and driven by Donald Healey and Capt George Eyston, it took a number of records including 500 miles at 153.14mph and 6 hours at 145.96mph. Using the 'streamliner' with a blown BMC C-series engine, Donald Healey achieved the flying mile at 203.06mph – and having cracked 200mph he hung up his helmet. Unfortunately, neither car exists today since both were victims of of salt corrosion.

Like the earlier runs, these successes made an impact at the time which is hard to imagine now. It was the sort of achievement which was featured in British boys' comics, complete with terms like 'ace' and 'tuning wizard'. When it came to the people who could afford to write a cheque for a 100-Six, however, it was a different matter and the car was not successful when it first appeared.

THE 100-SIX

When the 100-Six was announced in 1956, little had changed in the mass sports car market worldwide. In Britain, however, market conditions had changed dramatically after 1952. Immediately after the war the slogan had been 'Export or Die' and British cars accounted for over 50% of exports in 1951, but when factories reached full production the government lifted restrictions which had limited sales on the home market.

This turned a seller's market into a buyer's market almost overnight and, with new post-war models coming on stream, British specialist firms followed the French into oblivion. The sales of Allard, Dellow, Frazer Nash, Healey, HRG, Jowett and Lea Francis trickled away, while the promising Swallow Doretti of 1954, which used Triumph components under a body not unlike that of the Austin-Healey 100, was killed off when Jaguar threatened to remove its business from Swallow's parent company, Tube Investments, if it continued to make a rival sports car.

Launched in 1956, the 100-Six brought many significant changes to the Big Healey, notably a new nose style, a six-cylinder engine and an extended wheelbase allowing 2+2 seating.

By 1956, Sunbeam Talbot had dropped the Alpine, Jaguar had progressed to the XK140 and at long last MG was allowed to replace the TF with the MGA, which soon led the sports car market in terms of sales. Triumph had the TR3, which was a marked improvement on the TR2 and which sold in increasing numbers, while Austin-Healey production remained tied to about 5000 cars a year.

So far as the home market is concerned, the low sales of the Healey were no longer due to restricted availability, but because people did not buy them. Each major Austin outlet had to take several Healeys each year, and although they attracted interest they sold slowly. We look back at the Healey with a sense of awe but people saw it somewhat differently at the

Austin-Healey often engaged celebrity help with its marketing. Peter Ustinov – actor, raconteur, bon viveur and car enthusiast – was on hand for the 100-Six's US launch.

time. Young bloods may have lusted after one because a pretty girl was an inevitable accessory, but few could afford one. Those who could buy one as 'the wife's shopping car' tended to settle on the MGA, which was perceived to be more practical.

On the world market, Mercedes-Benz had introduced the 190SL, but it was not very sporty and its compatriots, the Borgward Isabella Coupé and the Volkswagen Karmann-Ghia, were also boulevard cars. The Chevrolet Corvette still struggled in the market and in 1956 only 3467 were made. Ford (USA) made the two-seat Thunderbird but that was always more of a 'personal' car rather than a true sports car, and it soon moved into a different market sector. An ambitious attempt by the American Kaizer-Frazer Corporation to market a sports car in 1954 had ended in failure, while a number of other American sports car projects failed to take off.

The only significant newcomer was Alfa Romeo in 1955 with the Giulietta Spyder, which began to make inroads into the American market by expanding the sports car segment rather than taking sales away from other makers. Alfa's GT models, also popular in the US, helped open a new market segment to which British makers were slow to respond.

With the MGA safely launched as a relatively inexpensive 100mph sports car and with the Healey's sales never fulfilling hopes, it was decided to move the

model into a slightly different niche of the market. The 100-Six was to represent the most radical change in the history of the Big Healey.

For a start, the wheelbase was lengthened from 7ft 6in to 7ft 8in, which permitted a roomier cockpit although on BN4 much of the benefit of this was lost by fitting two small extra seats. Space was found for these by cutting back the rear tonneau panel (which ate into the boot space), although when the two-seat BN6 was introduced the panel remained much the same as on the 100.

Under the bonnet was the C-series engine, which had originally been developed by Morris Engines for BMC saloons. An all-iron pushrod unit of 2639cc (77mm × 89mm), it ran in four main bearings and bore a strong family resemblance to the smaller A-series and B-series units, the stroke being identical to that of the B-series. When fitted to BMC saloons it produced between 86–95bhp, but with a higher compression ratio and twin SUs, 102bhp was available for the 100-Six.

By 1956, road tests were beginning to become a little uneasy about the boot space of a car that had been praised only three years before. In providing seating for two legless midgets, it was necessary for the hood, hood-sticks, tonneau cover and sidescreens to be stored in the boot which, in the case of all 2+2 models, also housed a single 12-volt battery that

'Miss Auto Show' at the 1957 Washington Show in the US with a sectioned display version of the 100-Six engine built by apprentices at Longbridge.

further ate into the luggage space. The battery was fitted with a master switch, which provided some protection against theft. On the original 100 the hood had been an after-thought, but the 100-Six hood was an improvement in that it eliminated draughts and, when erected, had a different profile. The sidescreens had one sliding panel, allowing a contortionist to execute hand signals.

Road tests complained that the horseshoe shape of the occasional seats meant it was difficult to lodge a suitcase on them, a criticism that remained until the 3000 MkIII. Two extra inches of wheelbase meant that the length of the doors increased by the same amount, so the overall style was virtually unaltered.

On the subject of doors, a friend of mine was once told by Donald Healey: "Fitting doors was always a problem, and if one didn't fit we put it to one side and fitted another. At the end of the week all the rejected doors were sent to dealers as spares!" Have you ever wondered why the British motor industry went down the tubes?

The chassis remained little changed. There were revisions to the engine mounts to accommodate the six-cylinder unit and, for the same reason, the radiator was moved ahead of the front crossmember. Weight distribution front/rear changed slightly from 50/50 to

49/51 and, since the overall weight increased, the Healey was thought to have lost some of its original handling sharpness. There were detail changes to some of the brackets and on the two-seat BN6 additional brackets supported the twin 6-volt batteries. From December 1957 the bulkhead area around the gearbox was strengthened to reduce scuttle shake, but it was only a partial cure and scuttle shake would become a target for stronger criticism as time went on.

DHM wanted to make a number of fundamental modifications to the design, but was over-ruled by BMC in order to keep the project cheap. The fact that no serious capital investment was ever made in the model became increasingly apparent.

Little was changed in the suspension and steering over the original except that the steering ratio increased to 14:1, although from July 1958 it grew again to 15:1 and remained so on all subsequent cars. At first BN4 had an adjustable steering column fitted as standard, but from September 1958 this became an optional extra, as it was on every BN6. In February 1957 slightly longer front springs were introduced on BN4. The rear axle remained the standard BMC three-quarter floating axle in a banjo case, as fitted to other cars using the C-series engine; cars with overdrive had a 4.1:1 final drive ratio, those without

At the front, Austin's corporate influence brought a new 'crinkle' style to the radiator grille, now broadened and flattened to form an elongated oval.

Originally used in BMC saloons, the six-cylinder C-series engine found another home in the Healey, but its initial 102bhp output was only a small gain over its four-cylinder predecessor – and its 142lb ft of torque was actually less.

In case anyone failed to realise what lay behind the revised radiator grille, the badge indicated the number of cylinders.

The 'Austin-Healey' nose badge remained unchanged from the four-cylinder cars, but the chrome-embellished bonnet air intake was new for the 100-Six.

Light-faced instruments were part of a mild upgrade to the dashboard. This style of Motalita wood-rim steering wheel was a popular replacement for the rather unsporting standard offering in black plastic.

The 100-Six's extended cockpit and 2in wheelbase stretch allowed room for 2+2 seating in BN4 form, although a two-seater BN6 was added 18 months into the model's life.

had 3.909:1. The new rear axle meant that the rear track was slightly narrower than it had been on the original 100.

With a power bulge incorporating a small air scoop on the bonnet (which fulfilled some of the function of a carburettor cold-air box) and a new oval grille which few thought was an improvement, the 100-Six was easily distinguished from its predecessor. Since the radiator had been moved forward in the chassis, the bonnet line was extended but without affecting the overall aesthetics. The bonnet was also hinged at the rear, and some 100-Six bonnets had a central ridge in

the power bulge. Less obvious recognition points were the fact that the styling crease (or 'swage line') extended behind the rear wheels, the fuel filler became external, the bumpers had a wider central groove and the glass in the combined sidelight/indicator units and separate reflectors was conical instead of flat.

While the windscreen, now in Triplex laminated glass, retained the overall shape of the original, and the frame was colour-coded with the upper bodywork, it could no longer be folded flat. Apparently windscreens had sometimes broken when being adjusted, resulting in unwelcome warranty claims. Not being able to fold

A 100-Six provides transport for Stirling Moss at Aintree before the 1957 British GP, which he went on to win for Vanwall.

back the windscreen undoubtedly affected the performance figures obtained by road testers.

Door handles appeared for the first time and some early models had an external lock (apparently old Jowett stock bought cheaply when Jowett folded in 1953) on the left-hand door. Not until 1964 would the Healey have lockable doors all round. Despite the addition of door handles, the inside of the doors remained basically the same as on the 100. Indeed, there was no significant change to the cockpit area except that the dashboard was finished in leathercloth and the chromed strip on the top of the scuttle was replaced by a padded strip finished in artificial leather. This apparent concession to safety was rather negated by the fact that the steering column on all Healeys was a spear waiting to pierce the driver's chest in the event of a heavy head-on shunt.

The heater, no longer standard, became an optional extra at £23 5s. The new heater, however, did have demisting ducts and a fresh air blower, which partially helped to clear the cockpit of unwanted heat from the engine. While the new model seemed little more expensive than the 100 with a price hike of just £12, when one added together all the items which had been standard on the 100 but were extra on the 100-Six, the difference was a considerable £139 10s.

A fibreglass hardtop with sliding perspex sidescreens became a £90 optional extra from 1957 and continued to be offered until the 3000 MkII Convertible, whose fixed hood made fitting a hardtop impossible. A fringe benefit of the hardtop was that it allowed the Healey to be classified as a GT car for competition purposes.

The other main external difference was that pressed steel wheels became standard, with 48-spoke Dunlop wires as an optional extra. From a practical point of view this was sensible since the 100-Six's extra weight put more stress on the already fragile wires, but most buyers opted for wires because they looked so good and many paid extra to have Dunlop Road Speed tyres. In each case the wheels were 4J-15, and the steel ones with chrome-plated hub caps were identical to those on the Austin A90 Westminster.

Cars supplied to Germany and Switzerland from August 1958 had octagonal hub nuts in place of the traditional 'knock-off' variety, which was the first sign of what would become wide-spread safety legislation to control the motor industry.

Despite the increase in power, the 100-Six's performance proved disappointing, not least because its weight had increased by more than 300lb. Top speed was the same as the 100 at 103mph, but the 0-60mph time lengthened from 10.3sec to 12.9sec, and all intermediary times were up as well with 0-80mph increasing by 4.5sec. For the enthusiastic driver, the additional weight and the 2in increase in wheelbase dulled the edge of the previously sharp handling. Only BMC could give a car 13% more power and actually make it slower...

While road testers continued to sing the car's praises, some nagging doubts began to appear. Heat from the engine began to be mentioned and

The Autocar twice road-tested a 100-Six. This car was the subject of the second evaluation, in 1958, because it was fitted with the uprated 117bhp engine.

Three 100-Sixes amid a hotch-potch of Abingdon-built cars, including MGAs and a 'Frogeye' Sprite, undergoing final finishing at the factory.

reservations were recorded about the ground clearance, head clearance when the hood was erected, and the fact that the pedals, which were now off-set to give a place for the driver's left foot to rest, were still cramped. References to the car being a sports-tourer, rather than a sports car, began to creep into descriptions. In a little over three years the perception of the Healey had changed.

Most of these criticisms were mentioned in passing, but Bill Boddy wrote in *Motor Sport*: 'On rough roads very vicious scuttle float and judder develop, which affects the steering column and conveys appreciable vibration to the driver's hands. On main roads this is not particularly evident but it is, nevertheless, something which no designer worth his salt would permit.' Scuttle shake was also a frequent criticism of the Jensen-Healey.

From October 1957 some cars began to be fitted with a revised engine and all cars from November benefitted from the change. As originally fitted, the C-series engine was restricted by a cast-in inlet manifold, but this was changed to a separate manifold with separate ports for all cylinders, hence the nickname 'the six-port' engine. At the same time slightly larger inlet valves were fitted, there were new flat-topped pistons which raised the compression ratio from 8.25:1 to 8.7:1, and larger twin SU HD6 carburettors, on a semi-downdraught manifold, replaced the original horizontal H4s. All the two-seat BN6s had the revised engine. When first imported into the US, cars with the revised engine were marketed as the 100-Six MM

– 'Mille Miglia' – in memory of the minor class win in the 1957 race.

Power increased from 102bhp to 117bhp, and torque improved from 142lb ft at 2400rpm to 149lb ft at 3000rpm. These improvements transformed the car's performance and character: maximum speed increased from 102mph to 111mph while 0–60mph came down from 12.9sec to 11.2sec. It was typical of the British motor industry that it took a year to get the car right – and never mind the buyers who handed over their clam shells for a machine which was neither as quick nor as enjoyable as the model it replaced.

Reading the road tests of the time, one begins to see that a certain disenchantment had set in. In most cases one has to read between the lines because not all magazines were as forthright as *Motor Sport*. In the US, however, *Road & Track* commented on the severe 'cab noise' above a certain engine speed, and said that all but the most gentle getaways caused the exhaust system to scrape on the ground, no doubt due to axle

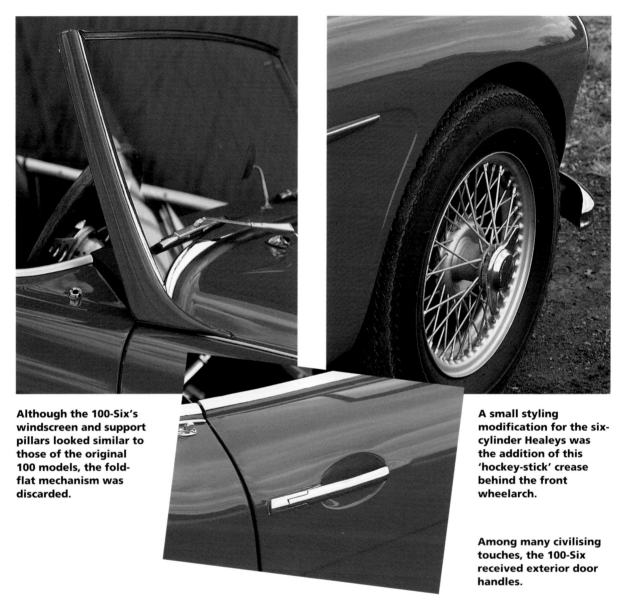

Although the 100-Six's windscreen and support pillars looked similar to those of the original 100 models, the fold-flat mechanism was discarded.

A small styling modification for the six-cylinder Healeys was the addition of this 'hockey-stick' crease behind the front wheelarch.

Among many civilising touches, the 100-Six received exterior door handles.

wind–up when accelerating hard. *Road & Track* went on to praise the car's handling, but panned rearward visibility and access with the hood in place.

The Autocar came clean about how tiring the Healey was to drive at speed because bumps and road camber affected its directional stability, and therefore a firm grip on the wheel was needed. With the hardtop in place, *The Autocar*'s testers suffered from fumes in the cockpit – which was to become a frequent criticism – and declared that the 'occasional' rear seats were a waste of space at the best of times, and having the hardtop fitted was not one of those times. It was

known by then that the two-seat BN6 was in the pipe-line, and the magazine commented that it would be welcome since some boot space would be restored.

Road testers continued to praise the Healey's style, reliability, performance and value for money, but even the most timid began to express growing unease about the boot space, the changing nature of the model, heat from the engine, noise, poor pedal space, the difficulty in erecting the hood in the event of a sudden shower, and so on. The stunning beauty of 1952 was becoming less of an object of desire and more like a wife with niggling little faults.

THE 3000

When BMC launched the 3000, it abandoned its usual practice of announcing a new model at the London Motor Show in October. Instead the car made its debut in March 1959 at the New York Show, which was a clear indication of priorities.

Conditions had changed a great deal in the seven years since the Healey had been launched. Car ownership at all levels had greatly increased and the sports car market was booming in the UK and other European countries as well as America. A number of small firms sprung up, major companies introduced sports models and there was a boom in kit cars.

In 1958, BMC began to sell the Austin-Healey Sprite, developed by DHM. Its cheeky looks and crisp handling won an instant following, even if it could only reach 81.5mph and 0-60mph took 20.7sec – although that was better than almost any British saloon car up to 2-litres. Priced on its launch at £678 (inclusive of taxes), it brought sports car ownership within the reach of tens of thousands of new buyers,

An optional hardtop, which integrated with the Healey's lines particularly well, continued to be available on the 3000.

and more than 350,000 Sprites and MG Midgets would be made over the following 21 years.

An American buyer in 1959 had some enviable choices:

	Top speed	0-60mph	Price
AC Ace-Bristol	115mph	9.3sec	$5699
Alfa 2000 Spider	112mph	11.0sec	$5355
Aston Martin DB4	140mph	8.5sec	$9870
Austin-Healey 3000	113mph	10.9sec	$3051
Chevrolet Corvette	128mph	6.6sec	$4017
Daimler SP 250	124mph	8.8sec	$3923
Jaguar XK150 (o/d)	132mph	7.5sec	$4762
MGA	100mph	14.2sec	$2444
Porsche 1600 roadster	110mph	10.5sec	$3650
Sunbeam Alpine (o/d)	103mph	13.8sec	$2595
Triumph TR3A	102mph	12.5sec	$2675

Healey interiors always appeared inviting: this 3000 MkI looks just as it left the factory, with **the standard Bluemels three-spoke steering wheel and seat piping in a contrasting white.**

This 3000 MkI is unusual for three reasons: its colour is Pacific Green (a rarely-specified choice), it sits on steel disc wheels (most **customers opted for optional wires) and it has the two-seater bodywork (four times as many 2+2 versions were built).**

By 1959, Triumph was making nearly three TRs for each Big Healey, and there was no mystery why. At $2675, the TR3A cost only $80 more than the prissy Sunbeam Alpine and only $231 more than the less potent MGA. Price was not the only factor, for TRs had assembled an impressive portfolio of success in international rallies. *Road & Track* said: 'The TR3 is not the fastest sports car in the world, nor is it the best handling or the most beautiful. It is, however, just about the best buy on the sports car market.'

That seems to account for the Triumph's popularity, but does not explain why the Healey did not put on sales as the sports car market expanded. The American writer, Rich Taylor, provides a clue: 'The Healey was somehow more of a, well…*middle-class* sports car than a TR2 and MG TF. It was a cheap Jaguar, not an expensive MG.'

Externally the 3000 was unchanged from the 100-Six, the major changes being mechanical. The C-series engine had a new block casting and was bored out to

The 3000 MkI was externally unchanged from the 100-Six apart from badging, but under the surface there was an enlarged engine and, at last, disc brakes for the front wheels.

But for this boot lid badge and a similar '3000' flash on the radiator grille, the original 3000 – 'MkI' is a retrospective designation – cannot be distinguished externally from a 100-Six.

Despite its enlarged capacity and altered construction, the 3000 MkI's 124bhp engine **looks almost identical to the 100-Six unit, and is still fuelled by twin SU carburettors.**

2912cc (83.34mm × 88.9mm). The 1957 revisions to the engine were carried over and the compression ratio was increased to 9:1, a sign that high-grade fuel had become readily available in Austin-Healey's main markets, although the best fuel available on the continent made the engine pink and over-run.

These small changes increased power to 124bhp at 4600rpm and torque to 162lb ft at 2700rpm. A new 10in Borg & Beck clutch replaced the previous 9in unit to cope with the increased power. Allied to a revised final drive ratio (revised again in March 1960), maximum speed was raised to 114mph with 0-60mph taking 11.4sec. Of perhaps more significance to most

Cutaway diagram of the 2912cc C-series engine, which used a new block casting, shows four main bearings and pushrod actuation for the valves.

Into the 3000 period, the American market continued to be very important for Austin-Healey. In 1959, the year this advertisement appeared in *Road & Track*, 5606 MkIs were sold in North America, yet only 280 found homes in the UK.

Autocar

drivers, however, was the fact that acceleration above 70mph was improved, so you did not need unlimited space to realise the car's maximum, and there were improvements in the really important speed increments, such as 50-70mph.

If the 3000 went better, it also stopped better thanks to 11in Girling disc brakes fitted at the front, nearly five years after the 100S had discs on all four wheels. Early disc brakes were prone to warping, however, and were less predictable than drums – Porsche was still using drum brakes in Formula 1 as late as 1961. By the standards of their time, all Healeys had excellent brakes and it was prudence rather than tardiness which delayed the introduction of discs.

In America, *Sports Car Illustrated* declared that the 3000 was the best Big Healey yet. Apart from the increase in power, there was better braking, improved gear ratios and the handling was sharper. *The Autocar* headlined the improvements in performance, while John Bolster of *Autosport* struggled to find words for his admiration of the engine's flexibility.

Overall, the car's shortcomings tended to be picked up with increasing emphasis. Poor lateral seat support was added to the list (previously it had been hinted), as was the seat adjustment. *The Autocar* praised the Healey's ability to cruise all day at 100mph on continental motorways, yet raised again the hot

The Austin Healey '3000'

ODDS-ON FAVORITE. The sky's clear, the air's like wine. You're ready for fun, and ready to go. And so is this spirited performer. The Austin Healey '3000' is the fabulous successor to the famous Austin Healey 100-Six which has dominated competition in its class. The '3000' hugs corners, clings to the road with sure-footed assurance. Has speed in reserve for a straight-away 115 m.p.h. Disc brakes bring it to a smooth, straight-line stop. Take this beauty out on the road, and you're really living. For as low as $3051 p.o.e. (2 or 4 seater).

The AUSTIN HEALEY SPRITE. The lowest priced true sports car on the market. Cleaned up in its class at Sebring. Top speed, 85 m.p.h. For as low as $1795 p.o.e.

Products of THE BRITISH MOTOR CORPORATION, LTD., makers of Austin Healey, Austin, MG, Magnette, Morris and Riley cars. Represented in the United States by Hambro Automotive Corp., Dept. 26, 27 W. 57th St., New York 19, N.Y. Sold and serviced in North America by over 1000 franchisees and dealers.

A pair of MkIIs together in 1961: the revised Big Healey, with a new radiator grille, strikes a publicity pose with its rebodied Sprite sister.

cockpit, the cramped pedals and the confined driving position which had been overtaken by the 'arm's length' style. For the first time a road test recorded how the Healey suffered from axle wind-up and tramp when starting in earnest from standstill, and how this affected acceleration times. Until the 1950s, road tests had often recorded 10-60mph times as the standard, which says something about axle tramp on earlier cars.

In Britain, a modified 3000 was offered by Ken Rudd, a Worthing garage owner who had made his name racing AC Aces. By using three SUs on a special manifold, a polished head and oversize porting, Rudd was able to extract 178bhp without using a high-lift camshaft, and offered works-style suspension modifications. Writing for *Autosport*, John Bolster recorded 9.6sec for 0-60mph, while 0-100mph dropped from the standard car's 32sec to just 21.6sec. Bolster made the point that the suspension revisions were essential and that caution was needed above 120mph, which he achieved on the new M1 motorway.

While justified criticisms of the standard car remained, the 3000 was greeted with more enthusiasm than at any time since the original 100 was launched onto an astonished market. It seems that the virtues of the revised design out-weighed its inherent drawbacks, and that the Healey had become accepted for what it was and not what its critics wanted it to become.

3000 MkII

The New York Motor Show in March 1961 was the venue for the unveiling of the 3000 MkII, which differed from the 3000 by having vertical bars in the radiator grille and bonnet scoop. Engines received a three-carburettor (SU HS4) manifold which boosted maximum power to 132bhp at 4750rpm. While maximum torque remained at 167lb ft, it moved up the range a little from 2700rpm to 3000rpm. This had the effect of improving the 0-60mph time to 10.9sec, but unfortunately the new system proved difficult to keep in tune and was used for only 10 months.

One wonders why the snag was not discovered before the car was sold, just as one wonders why the gear ratios on the 3000 had to be changed after 12 months when they had been praised so highly on the model's release, and why it was not until August 1961 that a brake servo became an option. If a brake servo was considered worth offering in August 1961, it must have been worth offering in March 1961. In its test of the original 3000, *The Motor* had suggested a servo.

To comply with local requirements, from September 1961 cars exported to Sweden and Germany had lockable steering columns which

A 3000 MkII Convertible in all its glory. Accompanying the new refinement of winding windows was a substantial chromed strip along the top of each door.

From this angle, the sharp crease along the MkII's new radiator grille shows up clearly.

The MkII's triple SU carburettors, which boosted maximum power to 132bhp, **proved difficult to keep in tune and were dropped after only 10 months.**

incorporated the ignition and starter mechanisms. It remains a mystery why only the Swedes and Germans should enjoy this convenience and security.

A different matter was a new gearbox, which was introduced on all cars from November 1961. The ratios were unaltered but the new 'box permitted a true central change with a short vertical lever rather than a cranked lever. Since it had a narrower casing than the previous model, this 'box also allowed more foot space around the pedals, thus addressing a persistent criticism.

Some improvements had been made to the fresh air booster, and now that the problem was partly solved road testers began to admit that high cockpit temperatures in previous models had not just been high, but unacceptably high. *The Autocar* became so emboldened as to point out that although the Healey's power had gone up from 90bhp to 132bhp, its weight had increased and the bhp/ton ratio had only risen from 102 to 117. Weight distribution was now biased more towards the rear at 47.3/52.7, which contrasts with the 50/50 of the original 100.

The Healey had been a great concept in its time, but it had been rushed into production without proper attention to design detail and these overlooked details were becoming increasingly unacceptable by 1961, when Jaguar was selling the E-type and MG was preparing the 'B' for production. *The Autocar* recorded its dismay that '...a company which has been

It looks just like the MkII Convertible from this angle but this is an early MkIII, which offered 150bhp and a more luxurious interior.

By the end of the Big Healey's life, the bulkier hood, quarterlights and larger windscreen made the shape look rather less lithe in profile than the 1953 original.

developing this series of Austin-Healeys for eight years, is still delivering cars with two familiar and quite serious, but demonstrably curable, shortcomings in respect of ground clearance and heat in the cockpit.'

3000 MkII Convertible ....

In January 1962 came the Mk II 'convertible', which was available only as a 2+2 since sales of the two-seat version had dwindled, largely because the buying public's perception of the Healey had changed over nearly 10 years. It featured a new curved windscreen with swivelling quarterlights, and was fitted with a fixed foldaway hood (with a detachable rear panel) and winding windows which eliminated the handy stowage space in the hollow doors, although elasticated map pockets were provided. Having a more sophisticated hood meant that the hardtop was impossible to fit, so it ceased to be an option – although the works rally cars continued to use them.

Instead of being colour-coded, the windscreen frame was chromed and there were chrome-plated cappings on the tops of the doors. Seats were no longer in leather but in a porous plastic with leather graining, and several colour finishes were available. White-wall tyres were also an option and were popular in America.

The tricky triple-carb system of the MkII was replaced by twin SU HS6s. This slightly cut maximum power (from 132bhp to 131bhp) and trimmed maximum torque from 167lb ft to 158lb ft, but it did not materially alter the car's performance since the torque curve was essentially flat between 2800rpm and 3700rpm. Road test figures showed an overall improvement with top speed at 116mph and 0-60mph down to 10.3sec, so one wonders by how much the slight curvature in the windscreen improved the aerodynamics. With the increased top speed, however, road testers began to question the security of the hood, a point which *Motor Sport* had raised in 1959.

From October 1962, cars supplied to the French market were fitted with 2860cc engines to fall into a lower excise bracket, but some later cars had the full 2912cc engine. Some later MkIIs also had a 9.5in Borg

Together with its revised hood, the MkII Convertible received swivelling quarterlights and winding windows.

The 3000 MkII on test with *The Autocar*, which was beginning to express reservations about "two familiar and quite serious, but demonstrably curable, shortcomings in respect of ground clearance and heat in the cockpit".

& Beck diaphragm spring clutch, which became standard on the MkIII and was generally thought to be an improvement, although there had been few complaints about the previous item.

June 1963 saw the adoption, at last, of stronger 60-spoke 4.5J-15 Dunlop wire wheels, which were less prone to breakage – and some modern owners of earlier cars prefer to fit these in retrospect. It had been known for nearly ten years that the 48-spoke wheels could break spokes during hard driving, but the trouble was that BMC had entered into a supply contract with Dunlop for 48-spoke wheels, and until the conditions of the contract were fulfilled it had to use them or face a penalty. The problem over strength is one reason why wires, standard on the 100, became an option on the 100-Six.

On the subject of wire wheels, the spokes were always painted silver-grey during the entire history of the car, although some chrome-plated wheels may have been fitted to exhibition cars. When modern owners fit chrome-plated wheels, it is an affectation. Any car so equipped which does not have cracked chrome is an indication that the owner has not driven it as it was designed to be driven…

Perhaps because the Healey had remained basically

unaltered for so long, *The Motor* was prepared to take it on its own terms. Its test commented that the problem of cockpit heat had been greatly reduced and said, 'Some enthusiasts feel that the modern, refined, open two-seater is insufficiently masculine to qualify as a sports car…the Austin-Healey 3000, despite a number of up-to-date attractions, is a strong-willed survivor of a more hairy-chested era.' That, I think, encapsulates the Healey's essential appeal.

3000 MkIII

March 1964 saw the arrival of the MkIII (BJ8), which carried over the style of the MkII Convertible at a time when the Healey had slipped towards the margins of the mass sports car market. Nevertheless the MkIII still sold steadily, and indeed sold more strongly than

the original 3000. But we are talking of only around
110 cars a week, and by now the MGB and Chevrolet
Corvette were each outselling the Healey four-to-one.
The Triumph TR4 was not quite as popular as the
TR3A, but sales were about double those of the
Healey. Triumph also offered the 'entry level' Spitfire,
which consistently outsold the Austin-Healey Sprite
and MG Midget combined. When the Healey first
appeared on the mass sports car market it was a major
player, but ten years on it occupied a niche.

For the British customer, the MkIII's cost was
eased by a reduction in purchase tax, but that had little
influence on sales. Many people saw the Healey as an
old-fashioned car which once had had sporting
credentials, but, despite a successful rally programme,
had lapsed into middle age. *Motor*, however, had taken
the car to its heart: 'Makes and models come and go
while the Big Healey gathers momentum…In its latest
form, the combination of speed, refinement and
character is still outstanding value…It is now a unique
blend of vintage sports car and modern
GT…Handling and steering are by no means

**Seen on test at the
MIRA proving ground,
the MkII Convertible
had a much-improved
hood for better weather
protection. With the
suspension compressed
on this banked track,
the exhaust system
barely clears the road.**

outstanding by modern standards, but better than first
acquaintance and many old hands would suggest, and
the car satisfies the sporting tradition by being great
fun to drive even if it takes time and knowhow to
make friends.'

Engine power on the MkIII was increased to
150bhp and torque to 167lb ft by using a new
camshaft, stronger valve springs, twin 2in SU HD8
carburettors and a new dual exhaust system with
additional silencers at the rear, making four silencers in
all. In conjunction with revised gear ratios, these
improvements meant a top speed of 121mph and 0-
60mph in 9.8sec.

The dashboard was also restyled with walnut
veneer panelling and a central console between the
seats. It seems that BMC had acknowledged the

Rear lighting changed, aesthetically for the worse, on the 3000 MkIII with the addition of separate indicators in the upper pods that had previously housed the reflectors.

The most significant changes to the Big Healey's interior came with the MkIII, which was generally upgraded to suit the car's transition from sporting to grand touring.

Among the interior changes, none was more striking than the introduction of a completely new wooden dashboard.

The nose badge announced the final Healey designation. Pedants may like to know that 'Austin-Healey' had mysteriously lost its hyphen when the MkII was introduced...

The 'Phase II' version of the 3000 MkIII brought a major chassis change to give more rear axle movement, but a less significant modification was the use of separate lamps for sidelights and indicators.

market's perception of the car and had made some effort to make it a luxury tourer. All cars had a key-operated starter, there was a lockable glove compartment, and the panel behind the obligatory '+2' seats could be folded over them to form a flat luggage platform.

By contrast to *Motor*'s enthusiasm, *Autocar* wrote: '…like an ageing but still beautiful dowager, repeated facelifts can no longer wholly hide the ravages of time and progress.' It not only repeated some previous criticisms, but noted that the new exhaust system was still unacceptably low, and that while it made the car very quiet at low speeds, engine noise made high-speed driving on a motorway excessively tiring.

Although the suspension had been acceptable on the car's launch, when sports cars were expected to have firm springing, by the 1960s it had become antiquated in terms of comfort and performance. Colin Chapman of Lotus had proved that the key to

good roadholding was a stiff chassis and relatively soft springing, yet the Healey soldiered on with suspension which, in essence, reflected pre-war thinking. *Autocar* complained that the car's hard springs and poor suspension movement meant that it could be knocked off course by bumps in the road when cornering, and that even in a straight line it was twitchy on any road with a less than completely smooth surface. In 1953 the Healey had been praised for its ability, comparative to other cars, to hold a straight course at high speeds…

Autocar also noted that the £2 8s 4d option of an adjustable steering column was fitted, but tartly commented that the adjustment would have been more useful had it permitted the wheel to be moved three inches *nearer* the dashboard because the driver was too close. Since the column was collapsible, it removed a little, but not all, of the danger of being speared through the chest by the column in a crash.

Only 1390 examples of the 3000 MkIII had been

A wintry press shot to mark the launch of the MkIII. Although radial tyres were an option and most owners now fit them, this car has crossplies, complete with the whitewalls which continued to be popular in the US.

made when there came the 'Phase II' model, which received the first major chassis change in the history of the Big Healey when the chassis sidemembers under the rear axle were dipped slightly to give the axle more suspension movement. It was perhaps the only lesson learned from the works rally programme that was passed on to the customer. At the same time, softer six-leaf springs were fitted and the lever arms of the Armstrong shock absorbers were modified to cope, while the Panhard rod was deleted in favour of radius arms which ran from the top of the axle to anchorage points in the body structure. This arrangement went some way to eliminating the axle tramp which had been a feature of every previous Healey. Presumably the first 1390 owners of the MkIII bought surplus chassis from the MkII production run…

Small though these changes were, they increased the Big Healey's appeal and the latter years of its life saw it selling at a greater rate than at almost any time before. The old criticisms remained valid, but the car's timeless beauty still turned heads. In America, where there was a 55mph speed limit on most roads, that was still a factor…

Ralph Nader's book, *Unsafe At Any Speed*, which centred on the Chevrolet Corvair, exposed the cavalier attitude of the motor industry to safety and environmental issues. As a result new legislation was passed in the US, the first measures due to take effect on January 1968. The Healey could not satisfy these requirements, so 1967 was its last year of production.

In January 1967, close to the Big Healey's demise, the market for larger sports cars looked like this:

The 3000GT was a fastback version styled by Healey in the early 1960s, but only one prototype was made.

Hard to believe, but there's a Big Healey chassis beneath this gorgeous Pininfarina four-seater body, which was built in 1962 to the winning design in a styling competition staged by *Automobile Year*, and revealed at the Earls Court Motor Show.

	Max speed	0-60mph	Price
AC Cobra 427	143mph	4.8sec	$7495
Austin-Healey 3000	121mph	9.8sec	$3565
Chevrolet Corvette	135mph	5.5sec	$4353
Jaguar E-type	139mph	7.4sec	$5385
Sunbeam Tiger	122mph	7.5sec	$3690
Triumph TR4A	109mph	11.4sec	$2899

Raw statistics do not tell the whole story. Among the things they obscure is that the much cheaper TR4A was a more practical and comfortable car than the Healey, and in real terms, driving A to B, it was quicker. The Healey's only advantage lay in high-speed motorway cruising (there was not yet an upper speed limit in Britain) and in its acceleration above 60mph. Even without the new American laws, it is doubtful whether it could have survived very long after the end of 1967, although DHM's proposed alternative, the Austin-Healey 4000, could have taken it into the 1970s because the shape remained one of the most beautiful in the world.

The Healey was the star of the 1952 London Motor Show and it has been a star ever since. True classic cars do not become classics with age, despite what some magazines try to say. True classics start with an indefinable magic. The Healey had it from Day One and there has never been a day since when it has not had it. What is it? That's like asking what was special about Rita Hayworth. If you have to ask, you'll never know.

The Healey in Rallying

The Healey became a rally car by accident. In 1957, a works 100-Six ran in an international rally for the first time when Tommy Wisdom and his daughter, Ann, came tenth in class and 83rd overall in the Sestrière Rally, a result which did not bode well for the Healey in rallying. After that one outing, the idea of rallying then appears to have been shelved.

It was also in 1957 that Healey production moved from Longbridge to Abingdon as part of BMC's process of rationalising its resources. Another part of that process occurred in 1958, when it was decided that all BMC's rally cars would be run from the Abingdon Competition Department under Marcus Chambers. Previously the group's efforts in rallying had been without a focus, and it showed in poor results. The move to Abingdon, however, meant that the Healey received attention from MG's team of first-class engineers, headed by Syd Enever, who really understood the requirements of competition.

Chambers had intended to enter a team of MGA Twin Cams in the 1958 Alpine Rally, but when the car was late coming into production – it was not much use when it did appear – it was decided to run 100-Six Healeys instead. It should be recalled that rallies were run on a class handicap system and that the winner was the car which won its class by the widest margin – which is why the Mini Cooper would be so successful. Four of the five works 100-Sixes finished the rally, but only one won a *Coupe des Alpes* and all were beaten by a Triumph TR3A.

A month later, however, came the Liège-Rome-Liège Rally – the *Marathon de la Route* – which was

The 1958 Tulip Rally was only the second works outing for a 100-Six. Jack Sears and Peter Garnier lay second in class behind a Mercedes 300SL, but UOC 741 later lost time with a broken distributor driving shaft.

The Abingdon Competitions Department moved on to 3000 MkI rally cars for 1959, when Jack Sears (below, at Zandvoort race circuit) and Peter Garnier managed to survive the Tulip Rally to take a class win in PMO 203.

Pat Moss (sister of Stirling) was the star Healey performer in 1960, following up her second place on the Alpine Rally (top) with outright victory on the Liège-Rome-Liège

Marathon de la Route (above). The latter was a significant landmark: it was the Healey's first international success and the first major rally to be won by a woman driver.

then reckoned to be the toughest event in the calendar. In fact it was virtually a race run in stages. Fourth overall, and ahead of all the Triumphs, came Pat Moss, and the three Healeys which finished won the Manufacturers' Team Prize. The Healey had found its role, although there is a certain irony in the fact that it entered its most successful period as a competition car when the road car was becoming regarded by some people as a rather dated tourer.

Pat Moss, sister of Stirling, was not only the best woman rally driver of her day, but she also has a strong claim to be numbered among the greatest rally drivers ever. Few drivers could get the best out of the rally Healey because it was nose-heavy, had rock-hard suspension, a slow gearchange and even its 6½J-16 wheels were skinny, but Pat was one of the few.

Apart from the fact that you had to be a hero, or heroine, to take a Healey near its limit, you also needed unusual stamina because of the intense cockpit heat, particularly when side exhausts were used from 1959. Pat told me that once she and her co-driver, Ann Wisdom, used to take it in turn to hang their feet

The best 3000 performance of 1961 came when the Morley twins, Don and Erle, won the Alpine Rally outright in XJB 876.

out of the passenger window. On one occasion, when they had time in hand on a rally, they were driving along a coast road and the sea was so inviting, and the cockpit so hot, that they stopped and plunged in. Their clothes soon dried once back in the car.

Extra vents, most memorably in the front wings, were added to cool the cockpit and asbestos lagging was attached to the engine bulkhead, but these measures only partially solved the problem. Since the works cars were not fitted with heaters, the cockpit, by contrast, could be extremely cold on winter events such as the Monte Carlo Rally because not even the engine and exhaust heat were enough to compensate.

Only during 1958 was the 100-Six used as a works rally car. In 1959 came the 3000 MkI, which picked up a few high finishes in rallies to demonstrate the model's potential. By then the MGA Twin Cam was a dead issue and development was concentrated on the 3000. Into 1960, triple SU carburettors and the famous moulded boot lid, which allowed two spare wheels and tyres to be carried, were further developments.

Once again, Pat Moss was the star performer and she followed a second place in the 1960 Alpine Rally with a win in the gruelling Liège-Rome-Liège. It was

the first time that a woman had won a major rally outright, the first time that a British driver had won the *Marathon de la Route*, and the first outright victory in international competition for any Big Healey. That win gave Pat a place among the greats of rallying and also made her name synonymous with the Healey, although she actually gained most of her major successes with other cars.

Early works Healeys were taken from the production line and modified. They were not specially constructed, although later cars were. In all, the works used 29 cars, six of which had begun life as 100-Sixes and been uprated to 3000 specification. Privateers tended not to prepare cars themselves, but ex-works cars trickled down to them and one was sold to John Gott, the Chief Constable of Northamptonshire, who was often a works driver.

In 1961, *The Motor* conducted a road test of Gott's car and discovered that it was more than 50lb heavier than the standard 3000. It was fitted with a blue-printed engine and the gas-flowed cylinder head had stronger valve springs. There were three 2in SU

You can almost hear the engine bellow. In characteristic Healey stance with tail squatting under power and wheels fighting for traction, Pat Moss's XJB 877 on its way to second place in the 1961 RAC.

The 1962 Alpine saw another major Healey success: the Morley twins won, but third-placed Pat Moss and Pauline Mayman (seen here) played their part in 77 ARX by helping to secure the coveted manufacturers' team prize.

carburettors and Laycock de Normanville overdrive on the top three close-ratio gears. Suspension changes included stiffer springs, dampers and anti-roll bar, while the semi-elliptical rear springs had 14 thin leaves. Ground clearance was increased by about an inch – a sump guard was still an essential item on all Healey rally cars – and the twin exhaust pipes exited just before the nearside rear wheel to avoid snagging the rear axle. Servo-assisted 11¼in Girling disc brakes were fitted all round.

The Motor praised the engine's flexibility: about 180bhp at 5200rpm was quoted at the flywheel and around 145bhp to the rear wheels, although these figures may be optimistic. The magazine said that, 'The touring character (or the ordinary Healey) has entirely vanished in favour of the hard, taut feeling of the sports-racing car'. Top speed was given as approximately 125mph, but it was noted that the perspex sidescreens were forced open at about 115mph. A 0–60mph time of 10.2sec was recorded, and not thought exceptional, but the 0–100mph time of 23.9sec was considered outstanding. In all, *The Motor* was extremely enthusiastic about the car, even if it had reservations about its handling in icy conditions.

The Morley twins, Don and Erle, who were farmers and did not compete at harvest time, took an outright win in the 1961 Alpine Rally and Pat Moss was second in the RAC Rally. At the end of the year, Marcus Chambers retired as BMC's competition manager and the position went to Stuart Turner, who had made his reputation as the outstanding British rally navigator and the first important rally correspondent, and who would later rise to giddy heights in the Ford hierarchy.

Turner brought to his job sharp intelligence, a thorough understanding of the sport and formidable powers of organisation. Coincidentally, BMC at this

Struggling for grip in deep slush, Timo Makinen's car understeers through Paddock Bend at Brands Hatch during a display rallycross organised for BBC TV in 1963.

time launched the Mini Cooper, which three years later in 'S' form would become the outstanding rally car of its era and would soon challenge the Healey.

The works Healeys in 1962 had three twin-choke Weber carburettors and aluminium cylinder heads, the latter, BMC declared, intended to reduce weight over the front wheels. It was, of course, merely a coincidence that the new head helped increase power at the flywheel to around 200bhp, or so it was claimed. A limited-slip differential was developed and Jensen supplied aluminium body panels in an attempt to reduce weight.

Successes that year included a 1-3 in the Alpine Rally (with the Morley twins winning again), second in the Polish, and second and third in the RAC. In events like the Alpine and the Liège-Rome-Liège, the Healey came into its own because its chassis and engine were incredibly rugged, and the engine's wonderful torque range was a deciding factor when

Autocar **managed 0-60mph in 8.2sec, 1.6sec quicker than a standard 3000 MkIII, in its 1965 test of DRX 258C. Three 45DCOE Weber carburettors were among tuning modifications which produced 173bhp at the rear wheels. Notice the detachable section of bodywork, a simple modification to allow access to the carburettors.**

The Morley twins in 1965 at an old stamping ground, the Alpine Rally, and heading for second place in the GT category in DRX 258C.

driving up mountains. Mini Coopers, however, won four major rallies that year because they were *comparatively* superior to anything else in their class.

With the Healey, Pat Moss won countless *Coupe des Dames* awards and the European Ladies' Championship for three successive years. Healeys were regular winners of their class and often took the team prize, and these were all important achievements at the time. It is this broadly-based record of success that has given the Healey its reputation as an outstanding rally car, since outright wins were comparatively few and far between.

When a Mini Cooper won the Monte outright in 1964, the writing appeared to be on the wall for the Healey, although Paddy Hopkirk took the Austrian Alpine Rally and Rauno Aaltonen won the last *Marathon de la Route* to be held on public roads, on this occasion following a Liège-Sofia-Liège route. There were also second places in the RAC in 1964 and 1965, the latter the Healey's last appearance as a works entry.

Autocar tested a works Healey in 1965 and

Businesslike interior of a 1965 works car, DRX 258C, shows matt black finish, electric windscreen demisters and the overdrive switch mounted on the large gear knob.

An evocative colour view of SMO 938 powering towards one of the greatest Healey victories, for Rauno Aaltonen and Tony Ambrose on the 1964 Liège-Sofia-Liège *Marathon de la Route*.

The Healey's last works appearance, seen in this rare colour shot, came on the 1965 RAC with second place for Timo Makinen and Paul Easter in EJB 806C.

recorded a top speed of 120mph, which was about as fast as a standard car. But 0-60mph was covered in 8.2sec and 0-100mph in 19.2sec was truly outstanding. It was in the intermediate increments, however, where the works car really shone over the standard car, with 50-70mph being covered in 7.4sec compared with 10.7sec in production form. *Autocar* concluded that the Healey 'has been developed into a classic competition car that behaves superbly on the road and well deserves to be classed among the all-time greats in motoring history.'

Few will seriously dispute that assessment, although in terms of outright wins the Healey, with five major victories, was overshadowed by the Mini Cooper S, which won six in 1964 alone. Healeys had presence, however, and for all their reputation for being difficult to tame, their drivers enjoyed the experience. They were probably the fastest rally cars of their era and offered an unparalleled challenge which only the best could meet. When the works cars passed into private hands they were not successful at the top level.

THE AUSTIN-HEALEY 4000

On 1 January 1968 the American government activated regulations which were to have a profound effect on the mass-produced British sports car. In the long term they would lead to strangled performance and rubber bumpers, and since the British motor industry would not, or could not, respond to the challenge they led to the demise of the mass-produced British sports car. The first to go was the Big Healey.

It was known that the Healey could not meet the new regulations, and the management of British Motor Holdings (as BMC had become after its merger with the Jaguar Group) decided that cost of a redesign was not viable on a 15-year-old model. The company was in deep financial trouble and the car was not a major source of profit, although the lustre it added to the Austin name was incalculable.

It was decided instead to cater for the Healey

The prototype 'Austin-Healey 4000', now beautifully restored, is instantly distinguished by its extra width and bulged bonnet.

buyer with the MGC, an ill-handling car whose chances were not enhanced by the fact that it shared the same styling as the cheaper 'B'. It used an engine which began life as a four-cylinder unit (made by BMH's Australian subsidiary) to which two more cylinders were added. The result met America's emission laws, but it was so heavy and poor an engine that the possibility of reviving the ex-Atlantic 'four' with a new cylinder head was seriously considered. Another proposal was that the MGC should be given a Healey grille and badged as an Austin-Healey, but Donald Healey flatly refused to lend his name to such an abomination.

Healey's preferred solution centred on the Rolls-

Badging gives credit to Rolls-Royce for the 4-litre engine under the bonnet of this fascinating 'might-have-been'.

Royce FB60 engine that was supplied to BMH for the Vanden Plas Princess *R*, an up-market variant of the A90 Westminster which failed to catch on. BMH had hoped to sell 5000 of these cars a year, but production ran at about a third of that number. Just as Donald Healey had been able to use the Austin A90 Atlantic's failure to his advantage in the early 1950s, so the Rolls-Royce FB60 looked ripe for plucking since penalty payments would be incurred if BMH did not take up its planned quota.

Further, Borg-Warner Model 8 automatic transmissions, ordered for the Princess *R*, were piling high in BMH's warehouses. Using these two major mechanical components in a redesigned car would allow BMH to absorb otherwise unwanted product. By then there was no pretence that the Healey was other than a tourer, so an automatic transmission was thought acceptable.

With two 2in SU carburettors, the Rolls-Royce FB60 gave 175bhp at 4800rpm and it was 100lb lighter than the C-series engine. Even with this engine in basic trim the Healey's performance would have been transformed, but Rolls-Royce was sufficiently intrigued by Healey's ideas to essay a double overhead camshaft cylinder head and one was made. With triple SU carburettors, it produced 268bhp. Even if we cut a slice from this figure to take into account the constraints of production and power loss through using an automatic transmission, we are still left with a sensational ingredient, and one which was considerably more powerful than the Jaguar E-type's 171bhp engine after it had been 'de-toxed' to meet American laws.

The Donald Healey Motor Company made a

proposal which was accepted in principle by BMH for production in 1968. A Healey was cut down the middle and the halves were set 6in apart, which meant it could accommodate the rear axle from the Princess *R*. At the same time the ground clearance was raised, which settled an enduring criticism of the Healey, met US rules covering headlight height, and allowed the fitting of an exhaust system with a catalytic convertor. Further, the modified body/chassis met new side-impact laws and the increase in width partly answered two persistant complaints: the Healey's cramped cockpit and boot space.

With an eye on upcoming regulations, the cockpit received non-protruding toggle switches and a collapsible steering column, and the wood panelling was removed from the dashboard. The fibreglass transmission cover was dropped in favour of a steel one which was welded to the main frame. This aided overall rigidity and, at last, eliminated the scuttle shake that every Big Healey had been heir to. It is a small point, but one wonders why it had had taken 15 years to implement so simple an improvement.

A combination of 'Phase II' suspension mods and a saving of 100lb in the engine resulted in a car with improved handling. The sharp edge of the original Healey 100 was restored. Even with a standard FB60 engine performance was sensational, and close to that of the works rally cars. To cope, disc brakes were specified on all four wheels.

Apart from the increase in width which, if anything, actually improved the Healey's already stunning looks, the other main recognition points were that the power bulge in the bonnet had neither an air intake nor embellishment, and there was a

A 1967 view of the Rolls-Royce FB60 six-cylinder engine fitted into the widened Healey. With two 2in SU carburettors, this engine gave 175bhp at 4800rpm.

Rolls-Royce badge on the boot lid of a similar style to that on the engine pods of airliners which use R-R engines. As flying became a familiar experience for many people with the potential to buy an Austin-Healey, this was a small but telling point.

Healey also produced a prototype coupé based on a 3000 with a rear profile not unlike a Jaguar E-type, but with a cut-off tail and vents in the wings which recalled, but did not copy, those of the works rally cars. It remained a design study, but indicates a possible option had the '4000' gone ahead.

The 'Rolls-Healey' or 'Austin-Healey 4000' was a delectable machine which did not proceed beyond three prototypes, for several reasons. BMH was able to negotiate its way out of its commitment to Rolls-Royce, so there was no longer the imperative to use the FB60 engines. Rolls-Royce had guessed that would happen and, having a stock-pile of FB60 engines, had disposed of some of the machine tooling – it would have cost BMH a lot to restore it. The MGC was on stream and was selling at Big Healey rates despite having received poor reviews. To judge

only from the balance sheet, it was an adequate replacement for the Healey.

Pitching the 'Austin-Healey 4000' into the market may have delighted potential buyers, but the cachet of a Rolls-Royce engine and similar power to a 'detoxed' E-type could have bothered Jaguar. Sir William Lyons, founder of Jaguar, had pulled the rug under the Swallow Doretti using his clout as a customer of Swallow's parent group, and it is not hard to imagine his reaction as a member of the board of BMH when his marque was threatened by the spectre of a revived Healey with better performance than an E-type *and* the cachet of two great names in Rolls-Royce and Healey.

Finally there was Donald Stokes, head of the British Leyland Motor Company which was formed in 1968 when BMH merged with Standard-Triumph. Just as Leonard Lord had promoted Austin to the detriment of the ex-Nuffield firms when BMC was

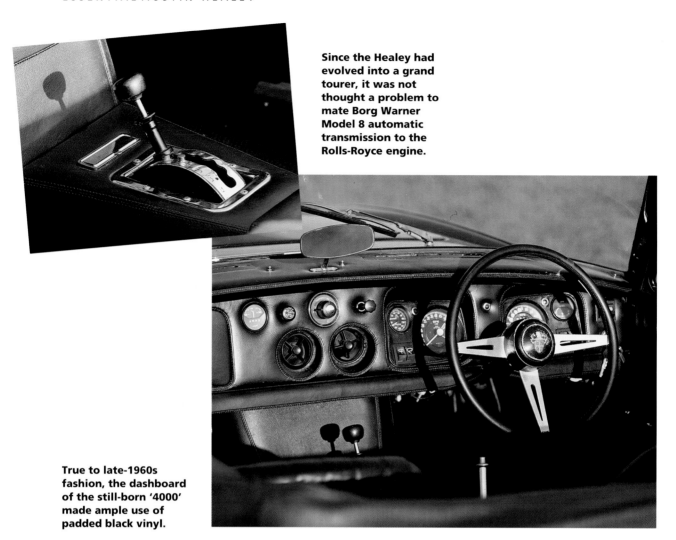

Since the Healey had evolved into a grand tourer, it was not thought a problem to mate Borg Warner Model 8 automatic transmission to the Rolls-Royce engine.

True to late-1960s fashion, the dashboard of the still-born '4000' made ample use of padded black vinyl.

formed, so Stokes promoted his background interests, which meant that Triumph would come to dominate Leyland's ever-diminishing sports car line-up. Stokes also decided that 'names' and competition successes did not sell road cars, so he axed the immortal Mini Cooper and saved the corporation the royalty of £2 per car it paid to John Cooper. Stokes' background was in truck building.

Donald Healey received similar treatment to Cooper. Stokes decided that the name 'Healey' did not shift cars from the showroom and it was dispensable. His own engineers, he decided, were more than capable of developing new cars – he did not need a little team operating from an outside factory. Years of reputation and goodwill went out of the window and the Austin-Healey Sprite became the Austin Sprite. Surprise, surprise, few people wanted to buy an Austin Sprite. And all this was obvious to

everybody except the most powerful man in the British motor industry.

The unique Rolls-Royce double overhead camshaft engine was used in a prototype chassis built by Austin which was given a stunning coupé body by Pininfarina and an Austin-Healey badge. The chassis was so incompetent, however, that the car was scrapped and – so the story goes – the engine was scrapped with it.

The Donald Healey Motor Company and British Leyland divorced and Donald Healey set to work on a new design which would become the Jensen-Healey.

One other thing. Two Healeys were imported into Japan, a country which saw few foreign cars in the 1960s. Both were bought by the Nissan Motor Company, which examined them in detail as an inspiration for the Datsun 240Z, which wiped the floor with mass-produced British sports cars in the US…

THE HEALEY TODAY

The first thing to say is that today we perceive the Big Healey in a different way from contemporary buyers. The Healey did not sell particularly well – even the MGC matched it for sales and the MGC was nobody's idea of a great sports car. After the excitement generated by the the original 100, subsequent variants were often seen as tourers rather than true sports cars.

In retrospect, however, any Healey is an object of desire because it remains one of the most beautiful cars ever made, and one which evokes its period like few others. The modern buyer is anyway looking for different qualities in a car compared with the buyer of 30 or 40 years ago, and the Healey will not disappoint.

In the late 1980s there was a minor UK industry in re-importing Healeys from the US and converting them to right-hand drive, but the madness which gripped the classic car world for two or three heady years – when cars were seen as marvellous investments which did not attract capital gains tax in the UK – has subsided. It is now possible to buy a Healey in excellent shape for the price a middling saloon car.

For the modern buyer of a Healey, the problems and pitfalls are the same as buying any other car over 25 years old. Rust is a major enemy, and when buying a Healey there are a number of particular points which should be given close attention. Replacement parts, however, are available and so comprehensive is the service offered by suppliers that it is almost possible to build a brand new Healey from spares.

Since many US cars have rusted less severely than their UK counterparts, hundreds have crossed the Atlantic in recent years. Triple carburettors reveal this hulk to be a 3000 MkII.

On the chassis, serious internal corrosion can occur along the lower surfaces of the main members and in the outriggers, particularly those which carry the rear spring shackles. The front crossmember should always be checked since it is vulnerable in the event of a head-on collision and can buckle if used as a jack-up point without a bearer to spread the load. The points where the engine mountings attach to the main chassis should be checked for cracking. If the chassis is past reasonable repair, it is possible to buy a complete new reproduction one.

The most notorious body problem is electrolytic corrosion where the aluminium bonnet and boot surrounds meet the pressed steel main body. Less well-known is corrosion on the front wings, most frequently below the headlights, along the lower edges of the wing panels and at the return flanges at the front of the leading door shut pillars. Rear wings most commonly corrode on their forward edges. Rust in the boot floor can often mean that the underside of the fuel tank is also affected.

Even when the outer shell appears to be free from rust, there can be decay in the inner body structure. The A-posts and B-posts can both corrode badly, and replacing them is best left to professionals because so much depends on their precise alignment, particularly with the A-posts. On cars without winding windows, the generous door stowage spaces can trap water and cause the bottoms of the doors to rot.

The good news on the mechanical side is that the engine of every Healey is rugged, although the four-cylinder can be a problem because relatively few were made and there are no reproduction blocks. Most other parts are available, and reconditioned exchange engines can be obtained. For those who wish to use unleaded petrol, it is now possible to buy a converted cylinder head.

Transmissions on most models are generally reliable, although second gear on the original three-speed (BN1) gearbox has always been a weak point. In general, however, most things which will wear on a car can be replaced or rebuilt fairly easily, and it is possible to buy reconditioned units.

Restoration of a Healey requires a high level of competence and is not to be recommended as a first restoration project. Undertaking someone else's half-finished restoration is rarely a good idea because it is likely that the work already completed will be sub-standard if a person has been unable to finish the project. Since experts expect to spend up to 1500 man-hours on a complete restoration, even a competent amateur working at home should expect to spend 3000-4000 hours.

When the prices of classic cars rocketed, some owners spent large sums of money on restorations believing that they were making an investment. In a more sober climate this means that excellent cars may be bought for much less than the cost of restoration. A classic car, needless to say, should never be bought as a financial investment.

Of the individual models, a BN2 in any form is sought-after, with a premium being placed on the 100M variant. Two-seat cars of any six-cylinder model are rarer than the 2+2 and therefore attract higher prices, while the 2+2 100-Six is generally considered the least desirable model. Just as the triple carburettors of the 3000 MkII proved difficult to keep in tune when new, so they are today. Most desirable of all is an ex-works rally car and most of these survive. Some people have converted standard cars to works specification, but the histories and locations of the genuine cars are well known in Healey circles, so a reasonably cautious buyer has no excuse for buying a car with a dubious provenance.

The strong and active owners' clubs in Britain and America can be of immense value in dealing with the practicalities of ownership, such as obtaining spares, and club magazines are a good place to find cars advertised for sale. Members tend to know each other's cars and discreet enquiries can pay dividends. In any case, joining a club before buying a car of this nature is a wise move because you can learn, before parting with your money, of all the pitfalls of ownership from fellow members who love their cars but are not blind to the problems of maintaining ageing machines.

For any European buyer, the USA remains the richest source of Healeys and a number of firms are able to convert imported cars to right-hand drive. The fact that all left-hand drive cars had the letter 'L' on their chassis plates is a point to remember, because not all conversions are of good quality. Advertisements sometimes lay stress on the fact that a car comes from California, with the implication that it has been kept in a dry climate and is therefore less prone to rust. Northern California, however, can be fairly wet and cars from the coastal area have lived close to salt water.

Dozens of small companies specialising in modern

The 'lookalike' Healey produced by Haldane is powered by a 118bhp 2-litre Ford Zetec **engine and drives through a Ford five-speed gearbox.**

versions of classics sprung up in the affluent 1980s. It was in this period that a company called Haldane made a 'look-alike' 100 with a fibreglass body, Ford running gear and Vauxhall Chevette front suspension. Haldane made 82 such kits which externally were fairly accurate copies, although, like most reproductions of early cars, the wheels were not quite right.

Haldane took the concept a stage further in 1993 and began to offer a range of 'turn-key' cars based on a spaceframe backbone chassis with independent suspension all round by coil springs and double wishbones. Power came from a 118bhp 2-litre Ford Zetec engine and drove through a five-speed Ford gearbox. It was a well-made car, although some of the classic car magazines wondered why anyone would

wish to buy one at about £19,000 when a real Healey in mint condition could be had for less. A good answer is a rust-free body and modern mechanicals: the car was aimed at a different breed of buyer who wanted Healey style without the problems. Among options were a 100M-style bonnet for the '100/4' model and rally-style side vents for the '3000' model. At the time of writing, Haldane planned to be able to replicate any style of Big Healey, including the 100S.

A more expensive proposition was the product of HMC (originally the Healey Motor Company). In 1990 HMC announced the Healey 'MkIV' and the 'Silverstone', which were high-quality evocations of the Austin-Healey 3000 with a fibreglass body, a 3.5-litre Rover V8 engine, a backbone tubular chassis, all-

An interesting view through the grille opening shows a four-cylinder 100's front crossmember, suspension and X-bracing.

Underside shows the basic Healey chassis construction, with two longitudinal members and a central cruciform bracing structure.

independent suspension and four-wheel disc brakes. A top speed of 140mph and 0–60mph in 5.6sec were claimed for both models, the difference between them being that the 'MkIV' had a more luxuriously appointed cockpit.

A body which does not rust, modern brakes, crisp handling and a decent cockpit sounds like the answer to a Healey enthusiast's prayer, and the late Geoffrey Healey – son of Donald – was happy to lend his name to the project. Jensen, however, still owned the rights to the Healey name and Jensen was undergoing one of its periodic revivals. A legal wrangle ensued and the name Healey had to be dropped. The early 1990s was not a good time to market a relatively expensive 'look-alike', regardless of its merits as a motor car, and at the time of writing it is understood that production has been slow, with most examples built to order for overseas customers.

APPENDIX

Extras and accessories ....

During the Healey's production life, a number of companies on both sides of the Atlantic made accessories such as wood-rim steering wheels, chromed badge-bars, exhaust trims, luggage racks, 'racing' wing mirrors and fibreglass hardtops. There was even the 'Plexidome', a clear bubble hardtop, although the last car which needed a greenhouse over the cockpit was a Healey. Today there is a variety of views about such add-ons among old car enthusiasts, who range from those who feel that period items add character to a car to those who insist that a car should be maintained in the form in which it left the factory.

In the case of the Healey, originality becomes blurred since BMC and the Healey Motor Company each sold accessories which are difficult to distinguish from those that were available in high street stores. The most famous add-on for the 100 was the 'Le Mans Modification Kit', but BMC could also supply larger fuel tanks, aeroscreens and wider (6in) wheels and tyres. DHM offered a longer list which included ancillary lights and instruments, leather cockpit trim, chromed rocker covers, air cleaners, badge-bars and luggage racks, wood-rim steering wheels, stone guards for headlights and ancillary lights, fitted luggage, radios, wing mirrors, a child seat which fitted over the transmission tunnel between the seats, fitted luggage and fibreglass hardtops with either a rectangular or wrap-round rear window. DHM also sold items which were identical to those on sale in the high street although they were stamped 'Austin-Healey'. What, then, is an original accessory?

When the six-cylinder cars came on stream, wire wheels, overdrive and a heater, which had previously been standard, became optional extras, although in practice most export cars were fitted with these as a matter of course. The DHM accessory shop seems to have declined as BMC started its own add-on business, BMC Service Ltd, which operated through the dealer network and offered the customer almost anything which a normal accessory shop could, including vulgar Ace Mercury chromed 'wire effect' wheel discs and

One of the most practical and popular options was a hardtop, seen here in two-seater style on a 100 BN2.

mock leopard skin seat covers. There were, therefore, two options lists – the one you ticked when ordering a new car and the officially approved accessories on sale at your local dealer – with a certain amount of overlap between them.

Factory-fitted items included the major units such as overdrive, but you could also specify additions like an external luggage rack, in which case a driver's wing mirror was always fitted. On the 3000, for example, you could have a cigar lighter, radio and a lockable petrol cap as original equipment. When the MkII Convertible came out the tonneau cover became an extra. And when the MkIII switched to Ambla leather-effect synthetic upholstery, real leather became an optional extra.

By such means the pre-tax price of the Healey – as with some of its rivals – was kept to a reasonable level and within sight of the 100's launch price of £750. We should not forget, however, that the 100 started life with wire wheels, a heater, overdrive and leather trim as standard, and it was not then widely perceived for items such as a radio and cigar lighter to be desirable in a sports car.

From the 3000 MkII of 1961, Kangol seat belts could be fitted without modification, and there was a kit to convert earlier six-cylinder cars to take them. Some well-informed drivers refused belts on the grounds that in the event of a heavy accident they preferred to be thrown out of the car rather than be strapped in place when the steering column hit them.

Production...

As has been noted in the text, it is not possible to be absolutely certain of the number of cars built at Longbridge (1953-57) because there was some confusion with other BMC models which shared the same running gear. I accept the figures quoted by Anders Ditlev Clausager in *Original Austin-Healey* (Bay View Books, 1990) as the most authoritative available for Longbridge cars. There is no problem with Abingdon-built models.

Authorities differ over the number of prototypes built by Tickford over the winter of 1952/53. Clausager says 20, most others claim 25, but my instinct is to go with Clausager if only because with BMC prototypes the lower figure is more likely to be correct. Some experts claim there were eight Special Test Cars (prototypes of the 100S), but since the works did not need eight cars for its activities, my hunch is to stick with the more usual estimate of five development cars.

I have not quoted figures for the 100M because Longbridge-built cars are included in the figures for BN2 while conversions carried out at Warwick included uprating existing BN1s. A full explanation is given in the main text.

Model	Years	Production
100 BN1 (3-speed)	1953-54	10030
100S AHS	1955	50
100 BN2 (4-speed)	1955-56	4604
100-Six BN4 (2+2)	1956-59	10268
100-Six BN6 (2-seat)	1957-59	4150
3000 MkI BT7 (2+2)	1959-61	10825
3000 MkI BN7 (2 seat)	1959-61	2825
3000 MkII BT7 (2+2)	1961-62	5095
3000 MkII BN7 (2-seat)	1961-62	355
3000 MkII Convertible BJ7	1962-63	6113
3000 MkIII (Phase I)	1963-64	1390
3000 MkIII (Phase II)	1964-67★	16322
Total		**72027**

★ Just one car was assembled during 1968.

A rare shot of a Healey fitted with a 'Plexidome', a clear bubble hardtop. On a car already inclined to cook its passengers, the greenhouse effect on a sunny day cannot be imagined...

Technical specifications ....

Caution should be taken when using the following information. It is believed that some early road test cars were supplied to the press in 'improved' form: they had some aluminium panels and tweaked engines. This might account for the excellent acceleration figures of the original 100.

On the four-cylinder cars there were choices of final drive ratios and also overdrive ratios, which naturally affected overall performance. On the four-cylinder models the windscreen could be folded backwards and this helped cars achieve a higher top speed than would be usual in ordinary road use. In addition, production standards were not consistent and the 'running-in' period was crucial. Some cars did not achieve the performance quoted for those supplied to the press. Later road test cars tended to be fitted with the optional hardtop which improved the aerodynamic efficiency. While the hardtop was popular, it remained an optional extra, as was an overdrive unit from the 100-Six onwards.

Figures quoted for weight are a guide only. Austin-Healey's options list was long and the weight of a car increased with an overdrive, a hardtop, mirrors, a radio, and so on. There could be a substantial difference between individual cars.

Top speed figures refer to the average of a two-way run.

AUSTIN-HEALEY 100 (BN1)

Engine In-line four-cylinder **Construction** Cast-iron block and head **Crankshaft** Three-bearing **Bore × stroke** 87.3mm × 111mm (3.437in × 4.370in) **Capacity** 2660cc (162.38cu in) **Valves** Pushrod ohv **Compression ratio** 7.5:1 **Fuel system** SU electric pump, twin SU H4 1½in carburettors **Maximum power** 90bhp at 4000rpm **Maximum torque** 144lb ft at 2000rpm **Transmission** Three-speed manual, overdrive on top two gears **Final drive ratio** 4.125:1 **Top gear per 1000rpm** 18mph (23.8mph in overdrive) **Brakes** Girling 11in × 1¾in hydraulic drums **Front suspension** Independent with wishbones, coil springs, lever arm dampers, anti-roll bar **Rear suspension** Live axle, semi-elliptic springs, Panhard rod, lever arm dampers **Steering** Cam and peg, first by Burman then by Cam Gears **Dry weight** 2015lb **Wheels/tyres** 4J-15 Dunlop centre-lock wire wheels, Dunlop Road Speed tyres **Top speed** 103mph **0–60mph** 10.3sec **Max speed in gears** 1st, 39mph 2nd, 60mph; 2nd (o/d), 76mph; 3rd, 103mph **Typical fuel consumption** 25mpg

The Autocar obtained a maximum speed of 119mph (111mph mean) by fitting the test car with an aero screen and running without a passenger.

AUSTIN-HEALEY 100 (BN2)

As for BN1, but four-speed gearbox with overdrive on top two ratios, and 11in × 2¼in front brakes. No reliable road test was conducted on this car and it is reasonable to suppose that performance and fuel consumption may have been slightly different to BN1.

AUSTIN-HEALEY 100M

As for BN1 except as follows: **Compression ratio** 8.1:1 **Fuel system** Twin SU H4 1¾in carburettors **Maximum power** 110bhp at 4500rpm **Maximum torque** 144lb ft at 2000rpm **Transmission** Four-speed manual, overdrive on top two gears **Top speed** 109mph **0–60mph** 9.6sec

The exact identity of the 100M is open to interpretation since any car fitted with the 'Le Mans' Tuning Kit could be classified as a 100M. Not all had the higher compression pistons, for example, which were usual when the kit was fitted by the factory. This means that some cars had 100bhp, not 110bhp, with a corresponding reduction in performance. See the main text.

AUSTIN-HEALEY 100S

As for BN1 except as follows: **Construction** Cast-iron block, aluminium head **Compression ratio** 8.3:1 **Fuel system** Two SU electric pumps, two SU H4 1¾in carburettors **Maximum power** 132bhp at 4700rpm **Maximum torque** 168lb ft at 2500rpm **Transmission** Four-speed manual, no overdrive **Final drive ratio** 2.92:1 (or 2.69, 3.66 or 4.125:1) **Top gear per 1000rpm** 26.6mph (with standard axle) **Brakes** Dunlop 11½in discs all round **Dry weight** 1700lb **Wheels/tyres** Dunlop centre-lock wire wheels, Dunlop 5.5-15 racing tyres **Top speed** 126mph **0–60mph** 7.8sec

As a bespoke racing machine, the 100S used a wide range of final drive ratios as a matter of course. Performance figures are the best obtained by road testers, but not all road tests produced similar figures. Works cars often used a four-speed Aston Martin gearbox and Dunlop magnesium alloy wheels.

AUSTIN-HEALEY 100-SIX (EARLY BN4)

Engine In-line six-cylinder **Construction** Cast-iron block and head **Crankshaft** Four-bearing **Bore × stroke** 79.4mm × 88.9mm (3.125in × 3.500in) **Capacity** 2639cc (160.98cu in) **Valves** Pushrod ohv **Compression ratio** 8.25:1 **Fuel system** SU electric pump, twin SU H4 1¾in carburettors **Maximum power** 102bhp at 4600rpm **Maximum torque** 142lb ft at 2400rpm **Transmission** Four-speed manual, optional overdrive **Final drive ratio** 3.91:1 (4.1:1 with overdrive) **Top gear per 1000rpm** 18.8mph (23.18mph in overdrive) **Brakes** Girling 11in × 2¼in hydraulic drums **Front suspension** Independent with wishbones, coil springs, lever arm dampers, anti-roll bar **Rear suspension** Live axle, semi-elliptic springs, Panhard rod, lever arm dampers **Steering** Cam and peg by Cam Gears **Dry weight** 2478lb **Wheels/tyres** 4J-15 pressed steel standard, 48-spoke Dunlop wires optional, Dunlop Road Speed tyres **Top speed** 103mph **0–60mph** 12.9sec **Max speed in gears** 1st, 31mph; 2nd, 50mph; 3rd, 73mph; 3rd (o/d), 95mph; 4th, 98.5mph; 4th (o/d), 103mph **Typical fuel consumption** 26mpg

AUSTIN-HEALEY 100-SIX (LATE BN4, ALL BN6)

As above except: **Compression ratio** 8.7:1 **Fuel system** Twin SU HD6 1¾in carburettors **Maximum power** 117bhp at 4750rpm **Maximum torque** 149lb ft at 3000rpm **Dry weight** 2478lb **Top speed** 111mph **0–60mph** 11.2sec **Typical fuel consumption** 23mpg

AUSTIN-HEALEY 3000 MKI (BT7/BN7)

As for 100-Six except: **Bore × stroke** 83.4mm × 88.9mm (3.283in × 3.500in) **Capacity** 2912cc (177.63cu in) **Compression ratio** 9.0:1 **Fuel system** Twin SU HD6 1¾in carburettors **Maximum power** 124bhp at 4600rpm **Maximum torque** 167lb ft at 2700rpm **Final drive ratio** 3.545:1 (3.909:1 with overdrive) **Top gear per 1000rpm** 18.94mph (23.1mph in overdrive) **Brakes** Girling 11in discs on front **Dry weight** 2513lb **Top speed** 114mph **0–60mph** 11.4sec **Max speed in gears** 1st, 34mph; 2nd, 49mph; 3rd, 78mph; 3rd (o/d), 98mph; 4th, 108mph; 4th (o/d), 114mph **Typical fuel consumption** 22mpg

AUSTIN-HEALEY 3000 MKII (BT7/BN7)

As MkI except: **Fuel system** Triple SU HS4 1½in carburettors **Maximum power** 132bhp at 4750rpm **Maximum torque** 167lb ft at 3000rpm **Dry weight** 2555lb **Top speed** 114mph **0–60mph** 10.9sec **Typical fuel consumption** 18mpg

AUSTIN-HEALEY 3000 MKII 'CONVERTIBLE' (BJ7)

As MkII except: **Fuel system** Twin SU HS6 1¾in carburettors **Maximum power** 131bhp at 4750rpm **Maximum torque** 158lb ft at 3000rpm **Dry weight** 2562lb **Wheels/tyres** Dunlop 4.5J-15 60-spoke wires became the option to pressed steel wheels during the production run; Dunlop SP41 radial tyres an option **Top speed** 116mph **0–60mph** 10.3sec **Typical fuel consumption** 20mpg

AUSTIN-HEALEY 3000 MKIII (BJ8)

As MkII except: **Fuel system** Twin SU HD6 2in carburettors **Maximum power** 150bhp at 5250rpm **Maximum torque** 173lb ft at 3000rpm **Top gear per 1000rpm** 20.72mph (23.0mph in overdrive) **Rear suspension** In 1964 rear axle located by radius arms instead of Panhard rod (MkIII 'Phase II') **Dry weight** 2604lb **Wheels/tyres** Cars exported to North America had wire wheels as standard **Top speed** 121mph **0–60mph** 9.8sec **Typical fuel consumption** 24mpg

ACKNOWLEDGEMENTS

Grateful thanks are due to the owners whose cars were used for colour photography. Eminent Healey restorer Gerald Stevenson supplied examples of 100 (BN1), 100-Six and 3000 MkIII specifically for this book, and Stuart Faulkner drove them for photography. Angie Cartwright's 3000 MkI (restored by her late husband, Eric, and maintained by son Richard) is the car shown on the front cover and elsewhere within the book. Other cars illustrated in colour were provided by John Wheatley (100 BN1), Ron Walker (100 BN2), Peter Ellis (100M), Frank Sytner (100S), Roy Standley (3000 MkI), Alan Taylor (3000 MkII) and Norman Pillinger (3000 MkII Convertible). Mell Ward (of the Austin-Healey Club) and Derek Mayor kindly guided us towards some of the cars. John Colley took most of the colour photographs, supplemented by work from Paul Debois. Sources for historic photographs were David Hodges, Autocar Motoring Archive, Quadrant Picture Library, John Bowman, Maurice Rowe, LAT Photographic and Otis Meyer of *Road & Track* magazine.